Social Service Delivery Systems: An Agenda for Reform

Cristián Aedo and Osvaldo Larrañaga
Editors
ILADES, Chile

Published by the Inter-American Development Bank
Distributed by The Johns Hopkins University Press

Washington, D.C.
1994

The views and opinions expressed in this publication are those of the authors and do not necessarily reflect the official position of the Inter-American Development Bank.

Social Service Delivery Systems:
An Agenda for Reform

© Copyright by the Inter-American Development Bank

1300 New York Avenue, N.W.
Washington, D.C. 20577

Distributed by
The Johns Hopkins University Press
2715 North Charles Street
Baltimore, MD 21218-4319

Library of Congress Catalog Card Number: 94-78312
ISBN: 0-940602-76-8

AUTHORS

Aedo, Cristián
Economist and Professor, Graduate Program in Economics, ILADES, Chile.

Garnier, Leonardo
Economist and Professor, Graduate Program in Economic Policy for Central America and the Caribbean, Universidad Nacional, Costa Rica. Member and Researcher, Alternativas de Desarrollo.

Hidalgo, Roberto
Political Scientist, Member and Researcher, Alternativas de Desarrollo, Costa Rica.

Larrañaga, Osvaldo
Economist and Professor, Graduate Program in Economics, ILADES, Chile.

Monge, Guillermo
Civil Engineer, Member and Researcher, Alternativas de Desarrollo, Costa Rica.

Rathe, Magdalena
Economist, ECOCARIBE, Dominican Republic.

Santana, Isidoro
Economist, ECOCARIBE, Dominican Republic.

Trejos, Juan Diego
Economist and Professor, University of Costa Rica. Member and Researcher, Alternativas de Desarrollo, Costa Rica.

FOREWORD

Latin America is undergoing profound economic restructuring. The debt crisis of the 1980s hastened the replacement of import substitution policies, which had begun to decline in use as early as the 1960s. Repeated financial crises in various countries and increasingly ineffective government monetary policies deprived state initiatives of credibility, thus justifying a reduction and realignment of state activities. The development plan outlined here is rooted in free market access, economic deregulation, and a more involved private sector.

The need for change in no way diminishes the historic role of the state in Latin America's economic development. Indeed, the state was the cornerstone of the industrialization process undertaken by the region's larger countries in the 1940s. In areas in which market forces have traditionally been inadequate, the state continues to play a role.

The state has also greatly influenced the social development of Latin America. Decisive government initiatives aimed at enrolling the population in education, health, and social security programs have helped to improve social indicators considerably. Despite these contributions, however, the countries still face important unresolved social policy challenges. First, the quality of social services is far from satisfactory. Second, rising public demands and limited supplies have created constraints on the funding and delivery of social services. Third, the crisis of the 1980s and its impact on social spending and personal incomes have increased the level of poverty in the region.

Moreover, several of the region's countries have relatively underdeveloped economies, with people living in extremely impoverished conditions. These countries face the urgent challenge of expanding coverage of basic social programs and alleviating the most extreme forms of poverty. The state has a vital role to play here, too, in aggressively promoting the process of social development.

Reform of the way in which social services are delivered is a necessary second phase of the ongoing structural change process. This reform is essential if programs are to be carried out efficiently and effectively. Overcoming poverty represents the greatest challenge to these countries in their aspirations to achieve long-term economic, social, and political stability.

Social Service Delivery Systems is intended to contribute to the discussion of these structural changes by sharing experiences and insights acquired in regional social policy matters. It aims at formulating recommendations that will make social services delivery responsive to criteria based on priorities, efficiency, and equity. Through case studies, the authors attempt to identify the best institutional arrangements for delivering social services. They pay particular attention to delivery mechanisms, decentralization schemes, private versus public delivery, and the targeting and efficiency of social policies.

The case studies deal with three countries with sharply contrasting social policies—Chile, Costa Rica, and the Dominican Republic. The Chilean study was directed by Cristián Aedo and Osvaldo Larrañaga of the Post-Graduate Program in Economics at Georgetown-ILADES in Santiago. The study on Costa Rica was conducted by Juan Diego Trejos of Alternatives for Development (Alternativas de Desarrollo) in San José. And the case study on the Dominican Republic was directed by Isidoro Santana of ECOCARIBE in Santo Domingo.

The first of the book's five chapters presents an analytical framework offering general guidelines for discussion of the reform process. The following three chapters contain condensed versions of each case study and deal primarily with the delivery of social services in health, education, and welfare. These chapters also present essential elements that should be considered when reforming social service delivery systems. The final chapter provides an overview of the study and highlights the main features of the countries' social policies, as well as related policy recommendations.

Nohra Rey de Marulanda, Manager
Economic and Social Development Department

CONTENTS

CHAPTER ONE

ASSESSING SOCIAL SERVICE DELIVERY SYSTEMS

Cristián Aedo and Osvaldo Larrañaga

Social policy is designed to help people develop capabilities needed for self-reliance, which is necessary if they are to escape poverty. The other face of social assistance is subsistence programs for those who live in extreme poverty or who are unable to work. How can social service delivery systems be made more effective in fighting poverty?

Financing and Sustainability of Social Policy

The effectiveness of social policy depends on its sustainability over time. Investments in human capital are long-term processes that unfold in progressive steps that include pre-school, elementary, and secondary education; neo-natal care; nutritional care; and health care for children and adolescents, among others. Moreover, welfare recipients also need to rely on a continuous and sustained commitment of support from the government.

Financing became a critical problem in the 1980s. Most countries had to curtail social programs because of budgetary constraints (Easterly, 1989; Chibber and Khalilzadeh-Shirazi, 1988), and the role of the state became pro-cyclical. Reductions in pensions and in other government assistance programs coincided with the deterioration in social service delivery caused by lower spending on public wages, procurements, and infrastructure. All of these factors worsened the recession's impact on human welfare.

Political, macroeconomic, and fiscal policy issues influence funding of social programs. First, the level of sustained spending over time depends on policy decisions—that is, how much society is willing to pay in taxes and what the priority uses of taxes are. To the degree that the decisions are based on a political consensus, continuity in social policy is assured beyond the term of individual governments and election periods. Second, the stability of fiscal revenues and spending is highly dependent on macroeconomic management. Attaining macroeconomic equilibrium, in particular, guarantees fiscal stability and enables economic growth—an essential condition for a country's social development. Third, the structure of fiscal policy is crucial in the formulation of long-term social programs and in the development of viable financing mechanisms.

In essence, an effective and sustainable social policy requires a solid fiscal basis that is rooted in economic growth, macroeconomic stability, and a political commitment to social fairness and the alleviation of poverty.

Decentralization

In decentralization, the central government transfers operational responsibilities for public programs to those closer to the beneficiaries. Often, such responsibilities are transferred to local governments, a logical choice since this allows beneficiaries' preferences to be voiced through local elections.[1]

Decentralization is a topic of current interest. It is the obvious alternative to current models of fiscal policy characterized by centralization, excessive bureaucracy, vertical decision making, and standardization of government programs and tasks. Centralization has been on the decline and has become increasingly ineffective as an instrument of public intervention. Decentralization, however, seems to be attuned to structural reforms that emphasize private sector participation as well as economic deregulation and openness.

There are strong arguments in favor of decentralization. When public policy makers live in the same area as beneficiaries, this ensures that the views of the latter are reflected in the formulation and implementation of public programs. Decentralized programs allow a greater diversity of public activities and are more responsive to the specific needs of individuals. Decentralization also encourages and strengthens community participation—a desirable end in itself—and encourages efficiency by fostering competition among different suppliers. Citizens would choose to reside in communities where desired services are being provided at the least cost (Tiebout, 1956).

However, decentralization also presents risks and problems. It could heighten regional inequalities by depriving the poorest areas of fiscal transfers from high-income areas. Revenue redistribution within regional communities would also be impaired because generous benefit programs in one area would encourage inflows of needy people from other areas. At the same time, the well-to-do within the community would move to relatively higher-developed areas. This could weaken the financial viability of the decentralization process over the long term (Blank, 1983).

---

[1] This constitutes the field of fiscal federalism that comprises raising fiscal revenues and intergovernmental transfers. Shah (1991) has provided a current review of the topic.

Additionally, a decentralization process could prove burdensome if it requires each community to undertake tasks that might be more efficiently carried out at the central level. Existing economies of scale should therefore be taken into consideration when dividing responsibilities between central and local authorities. The externalities that arise when providing public or free benefits may also cause problems. In this scenario, local authorities concern themselves exclusively with the welfare of their own constituents, without taking into consideration the impact that their resource allocation decisions could have on the citizens of other communities. Thus, a traditional argument (Samuelson, 1954 and 1955; Laffont, 1988) points out that such an approach would result in an inefficient allocation of resources. The Oates (1972) decentralization theorem, however, postulates that each public service should be provided by the jurisdiction covering the smallest geographic area, subject to the condition that that jurisdiction can internalize the benefits and costs associated with the services provided.

The lack of technical, organizational, and other capabilities at the regional level has impaired the decentralization process begun by several Latin American countries in the 1980s (Campbell, Peterson, and Brakarz, 1991). But this is changing. Therefore, as positions at local levels of government take on greater responsibilities and higher pay, they will attract more qualified and capable individuals than in the past.

Local democratic election mechanisms will help integrate constituency preferences into the process of providing public goods and services at the local level. The numerous local decisions regarding public income and expenditures could, however, run contrary to macroeconomic policy goals.

In summary, decentralization is an instrument with the potential to increase community participation and welfare services. Yet, a poorly formulated process could be ineffective, unfair, and contrary to national policy. Decentralization, therefore, is not a panacea that guarantees overcoming central government shortfalls. The success or failure of a decentralization program will depend on the characteristics of individual countries—that is, local versus central capabilities, program design, intensity and pace of reforms, redistribution programs between communities, and so forth.

Effectiveness of Public Management

Effective public management involves two objectives: (1) generation of a range of services at the lowest possible cost, and (2) delivery of a product that is a reflection of beneficiaries' preferences. The private provision of goods or services under free-market competition assures that these objectives can be met. The problem lies in how to ensure that the same efficiency criteria apply to public delivery of social services. For the most part, solving this problem depends on the ability of various public institutions to provide the most benefit to the community at the least cost.

One way of dealing with the problem is to rely on the public sector's organizational and incentive structures and to devise the means whereby a central government agency may control the quality of service deliveries provided by a local agency. This is related to the "agency-principal problem" that has been widely treated in the economic literature of the last decade (Laffont, 1989). The analytical solution to this problem lies in designing an incentive structure that ensures that the "agent" (i.e., local agency) fulfills the "principal's" (i.e., central government's) objective. However, this solution is difficult to apply in the public sector, where multiple principals exist (e.g., the public itself, the legislature, the office of the comptroller, etc.) and market shortcomings abound (e.g., poor information flows, tariff barriers).

Moreover, the efficiency and effectiveness of programs for transferring public resources from the central government to service providers depend on the transfer mechanism chosen. Different approaches could include delivery of fixed resource allocations without requiring matching contributions from the recipient, with the transfer being made on the basis of historical criteria or direct negotiations; transfers based on inputs, whereby resources are delivered in proportion to the level of inputs used in producing the service; transfers based on results (i.e., on end products generated by the program); and, finally, transfers delivered directly to program beneficiaries (demand subsidies).[2]

It is clear that transfers involving fixed allocations do not foster efficiency in service production nor do they engender consideration of beneficiaries' preferences. Moreover, such arrangements are subject to discretionary decisions and provide little transparency. Transfers based on input use or results do not necessarily guarantee efficiency nor are they responsive to demand; they might even encourage overproduction of services. These transfers, however, are more satisfactory because of their objectivity and transparency. In theory, a demand subsidy system represents an ideal approach, however, because it is market-driven and thus enables the integration of productive efficiency with beneficiary preferences.

Efficiency in public management is generally enhanced when the opinions of beneficiaries are taken into account. In this regard, Paul (1991) expands the concepts of "exit" and "voice," which Hirschman (1970) introduced into the field of public service delivery. "Exit" is the beneficiaries' ability to change suppliers when dissatisfied with a service, and "voice" is their ability to exert political or group pressure when dissatisfied with the service. The option of

---

[2] For a detailed analysis of this issue in the context of higher education, see Albretch and Ziderman (1992).

exercising both is determined by the implied benefits and costs of the activities. For example, the option of exercising both exit and voice in the supply of education within rural areas is slim because of a lack of supply alternatives (economies of scale, spatial barriers) and the low political leverage of the beneficiaries (geographic dispersion). On the other hand, the supply of education in urban areas is associated with a higher exit level insofar as (1) schools' financing in urban areas depends on their enrollment sizes and (2) schools internalize both the benefits of being selected and the costs of being rejected by families.

Targeting

One of the major issues in the area of social policy relates to the targeting of social spending—the delivery of subsidized social services to specific segments of the population and, in particular, to those living in poverty. Such a policy is selective and should be contrasted with universal policies that benefit all citizens and are characteristic of welfare states. One area that clearly illustrates the difference between both types of policies is higher education. Proponents of targeted social spending find in higher education the ultimate example of a program that should not be subsidized, since it would mostly benefit young people from wealthy families (Birdsall and James, 1990). Yet, higher education in a welfare state is subsidized and unrestricted (Rose and Shiratori, 1986).

There is no clear-cut separation between universal and targeted spending. In most countries, the state provides free elementary education to its population regardless of the students' socioeconomic backgrounds or the degree of targeting involved in other social programs. Economists explain the situation in terms of related externalities: the benefits of knowing how to read, write, and perform basic mathematics affect not only the student but also the people around him, thus justifying the subsidy of that activity. Moreover, access to basic education is a constitutional right in most countries. This concept is discussed by Okun (1975), who distinguishes between economic goods and individual rights. While the former are marketable, the latter are guaranteed by society regardless of individual income. Therefore, if basic education constitutes a right, then it is the responsibility of the state to guarantee its provision. Individuals who choose to pay for alternative services may do so through private suppliers.[3]

Philosophical considerations aside, targeting is often a consequence of fiscal constraints. This means that the government determines the content and scope of public programs subject to fiscal constraints that depend on external factors. In this context, targeting simply means allocating scarce fiscal resources to the highest priority goals.

---

[3] Extreme views exist that deny such a possibility.

In any event, targeting entails costs that should be evaluated along with its benefits. While benefits stem from savings of fiscal resources because of greater efficiency in spending allocations, costs result from administrative expenditures associated with selecting the beneficiary groups and monitoring program spending.[4] The convergence of benefits and costs determines the scope and nature of the targeting schemes. Therefore, if most of the population is poor, but appropriate administrative and data systems have not been developed, targeting should be avoided. In some instances, an intermediate option may be chosen whereby the target beneficiaries are selected on the basis of easily identifiable characteristics (e.g., age, area of residence, etc.), even when these characteristics might not provide the same result obtained from a proper targeting process (Besley, 1989; Keen, 1982; and Besley and Kanbur, 1988).

The state often provides universal public health and education services, at the same time that those services are provided by private sources at higher cost and of superior quality. In these cases, targeting is a result of the self-selection process of beneficiaries. Individuals of greater means typically prefer to acquire private services that are better, more convenient, and more selective.

Self-selection in social programs could be an implicit targeting mechanism. Thus, when detailed data on the beneficiaries' characteristics is lacking, the government could achieve targeting by charging a fee for benefits. This cost should be adjusted according to individual incomes in such a way that it would be advantageous for only the poor to enroll in the program. For example, it has been proposed that recipients of financial subsidies be required to work in exchange for benefits in order to self-select those with low opportunity costs (Besley and Coate, 1992b). In some cases, the beneficiaries' self-esteem acts as a filter, since the cost they must be willing to pay to access the programs targeting the "poor" becomes a self-assessment of personal worth (Moffitt, 1983; Besley and Coate, 1992a).

Economists maintain that the reason for providing subsidies in the form of services (e.g., education and health) rather than cash is that some system of self-selection is needed.[5] In the face of insufficient information it is difficult to achieve a truly efficient social program, and policy discussions therefore focus on trying simply to approximate an optimal solution. In this context, it may be reasonable to provide subsidies in kind that directly benefit the target group, thereby avoiding financial losses related to the provision of cash subsidies (Guesnerie and Roberts, 1984; Blackorby and Donaldson, 1988).

---

[4] Appropriate targeting, furthermore, minimizes the possible negative impacts of social policy such as dependency and dysfunctional behavior, among others.

[5] This is just as the principle of consumer choice would suggest.

Private Service Delivery

Private delivery of social services funded by the state has recently been recommended by several authors (Roth, 1987; Allen, *et al.,* 1989). Such recommendations are primarily based on considerations of efficiency—that is, on the assumption that the private sector can provide social services more efficiently than the public sector.[6] Private activities, including for-profit activities, can be perfectly compatible with the efficient production of social services.

Private sector participation can occur in two ways. First, the government can subcontract inputs or stages in the production of a social service. Second, the private sector can provide the entire service through a system of direct demand subsidies. In this case, private suppliers compete with each other for potential beneficiaries of social services.

In the final analysis, the comparative advantages of private versus public production of a social service will depend on the particular conditions of individual economies. This is an issue, therefore, in which decisions should be based on a careful analysis of those conditions. See Inman (1987) for a review of market shortcomings versus state shortcomings.

Another issue related to private delivery of social services is the need for public regulation. Education and health delivery are especially affected by major problems related to uneven or incomplete information (Barr, 1992). In this case, government involvement is needed either for providing information that otherwise would be unavailable or for penalizing any improper advantages derived from inside information.

Cost Recovery

The topic of cost recovery or payment for social services has recently been discussed by several authors (see in particular Jiménez, 1987). Basically, the arguments are related to efficiency. First, charging for social services would increase fiscal resources and enable the establishment of new public infrastructures in areas in which high rates of return could be attained. This is consistent with greater efficiency in resource allocations. Second, charging for service deliveries would concentrate on the demands of those beneficiaries who show greater propensity to pay for the services, reflecting greater appreciation for the service. Third, establishing a price structure would enable suppliers to determine the relative profitability of different social services, which would improve efficiency in resource allocations.

---

6 Public sector efficiency can be impaired by factors such as lack of incentives, excessive bureaucracy, political cronyism, and so on.

Nevertheless, it is clear that social service delivery is subject to externalities, lack of competition among beneficiaries, and, above all, considerations of fairness. For these reasons, user fees do not imply full recovery of service production costs. Subsidies could assist in cost recovery, which is certainly quite different from offering the service totally free of charge.

Ensuring Complementary Programs

Household behavior should be reviewed when assessing social programs since many important decisions are made by households that affect programs for the poor (Behrman, 1990).

Traditional economic theory makes a clear distinction between production and consumption. Production activities are carried out by companies, while consumption activities belong to the realm of households or individuals. Companies sell finished products (goods and services) to households in exchange for inputs (work and capital). The validity of these concepts began to be questioned in the 1960s. According to later views (Becker, 1965), the source of welfare lies in consumption "activities," not in the goods and services themselves.

In the household model, parents make decisions on basic allocations in an effort to secure maximum benefits for the household. These benefits are related both to consumption of "activities" (using market goods and services as inputs) and to the time and quality of each household member's human resources. It is assumed that parents try to achieve the maximum well-being for their families within the context of available income (the value of all resources on which the household relies, plus total transfers received) and the household's production functions (which relate to the goods produced by the family "activities").

One part of these "activities" produced by the household is the health condition of its members. This condition is evaluated on the basis of production functions that relate inputs—technical and biological—to the health condition of each household member. Some of these inputs are endogenous to the household (e.g., the quantity of proteins and calories consumed daily or the time dedicated by the mother and children to the production of the "activity"), while others are caused by factors exogenous or predetermined for the household (e.g., the educational level of the parents).

This type of analysis allows the evaluation of potential interactions between inputs, some of which may become guides for policy making. For example, the level of nutritional education of the mother (who is generally the one making critical health decisions for the household) affects food distribution programs for children. There are also indirect effects that cannot be included within this framework. For example, better health conditions of income earners within the household can increase their productivity, which in turn results in greater income for the family. This income could then be used to increase the family's demand for health inputs.

Understanding these interactions and any associated indirect effects is essential if appropriate social policies are to be formulated. For example, there is a two-fold relationship between nutrition and health. On the one hand, a nutritional program enables individuals to improve their health because of increased input allocations to such activity. On the other hand, the degree of use of these inputs depends on the individuals' health conditions. Moreover, a hygiene policy in the home increases the effectiveness of nutritional programs by diminishing the probability of infectious diseases.

BIBLIOGRAPHY

Albretch, D., and A. Ziderman. 1992. Financing Universities in Developing Countries. Washington, D.C.: The World Bank. PHREE Background Paper No. 61.

Allen, J.W. 1989. *The Private Sector in State Service Delivery: Examples of Innovative Practices*. Washington, D.C.: The Urban Institute Press.

Barr, N. 1992. Economic Theory and the Welfare State: a Survey and Interpretation. *Journal of Economic Literature* 30 (2):741-803.

Becker, G. 1965. A Theory of the Allocation of Time. *Economic Journal* 75 (9):493-517.

Behrman, J. 1990. *The Action of Human Resources and Poverty on One Another: What We Have Yet to Learn*. LMSM Working Paper No. 74.

Besley, T. 1989. Means Testing versus Universal Provision in Poverty Alleviation Programmes. *Economica* 57 (5):119-129.

Besley, T., and R. Kanbur. 1988. Food Subsidies and Poverty Alleviation. *The Economic Journal* 98 (9):701-719.

Besley, T., and S. Coate. 1992a. Understanding Welfare Stigma: Taxpayer Resentment and Statistical Discrimination. *Journal of Public Economics* 48 (No. 2):165-183.

————. 1992b. Workfare versus Welfare: Incentives Arguments for Work Requirements in Poverty Alleviation Programs. *American Economic Review* 82 (3):249-261.

Birdsall, N., and E. James. 1990. *Efficiency and Equity in Social Spending: How and Why Governments Misbehave*. PPR Working Papers (5). Washington, D.C.: The World Bank.

Blackorby, C., and D. Donaldson. 1988. Cash versus Kind, Self-Selection, and Efficient Transfers. *American Economic Review* 78 (4):691-701.

Blank, R. 1983. Welfare, Wages and Migration. Princeton, N.J.: Princeton University. Mimeo.

Campbell, T., G. Peterson, and J. Brakarz. 1991. Decentralization to Local Governments in LAC: National Strategies and Local Responses in Planning Spending and Management. Washington, D.C.: The World Bank. LAC Technical Department (No. 5).

Chibber, A., and J. Khalilzadeh-Shirazi. 1988. *Public Finances in Adjustment Programs.* PPR Working Papers (12). Washington, D.C.: The World Bank.

Easterly, W. 1989. *Fiscal Adjustment and Fiscal Financing during the Debt Crisis.* PPR Working Papers (1). Washington, D.C.: The World Bank.

Guesnerie, R., and K. Roberts. 1984. Effective Policy Tools and Quantity Controls. *Econometrica* 52(1):59-86.

Hirschman, A. 1970. *Exit, Voice and Loyalty.* Cambridge, MA: Harvard University Press.

Inman, R. 1987. Markets, Governments and the New Political Economy. In *Handbook of Public Economics,* Vol 2., eds. Auerbach and Feldstein. Amsterdam: North-Holland.

Jiménez, E. 1987. *Pricing Policy in the Social Sectors.* Washington, D.C.: The World Bank.

Keen, M. 1982. Needs and Targeting. *Economic Journal* 102 (1):67-79.

Laffont, J.J. 1988. *Fundamentals of Public Economics.* Cambridge, MA: The MIT Press.

———. 1989. *The Economics of Uncertainty and Information.* Cambridge, Mass.: The MIT Press.

Moffitt, R. 1983. An Economic Model of Welfare Stigma. *American Economic Review* 73 (No. 5): 1023-1035.

Oates, W. 1972. *Fiscal Federalism.* New York: Harcourt, Brace, Jovanovich.

Okun, A. 1975. *Equality and Efficiency: The Big Trade Off.* Washington, D.C.: Brookings Institution.

Paul, S. 1991. *Accountability in Public Services. Exit, Voice and Capture.* PPR Working Papers (3). Washington, D.C.: The World Bank.

Rose, R. and R. Shiratori. 1986. T*he Welfare State East and West*. New York: Oxford University Press.

Roth, G. 1987. *The Private Provision of Public Services in the Developing Countries*. New York: Oxford University Press.

Samuelson, P. 1954. The Pure Theory of Public Expenditure. *Review of Economics and Statistics* 36 (November): 387-389.

————. 1955. Diagramatic Exposition of a Theory of Public Expenditure. *Review of Economics and Statistics* 37 (November):350-356.

Shah, A. 1991. *Perspectives on the Design of Intergovernmental Fiscal Relations*. PPR Working Papers (7). Washington, D.C.: The World Bank.

Tiebout, C.M. 1956. A Pure Theory of Local Expenditure. *Journal of Political Economy* 64 (October): 416-424.

CHAPTER TWO

THE CHILEAN EXPERIENCE*

Cristián Aedo and Osvaldo Larrañaga

The purpose of this study is to draw economic policy lessons from Chile's social policy experiences.[1] Accordingly, the study describes the country's social programs in health, education, financial assistance, and nutrition and discusses the results of an econometric evaluation of quality and demand in Chile's elementary education system.

Chile's experience with social policy reforms is an invaluable test case because the country has dealt with the major issues involved—targeting, decentralization, private delivery, cost recovery, and demand subsidies—for over a decade.

The broad nature of the subject makes it desirable to be selective in choosing topics. Therefore, the study limits its focus to a current and concise analysis of the country's social programs. Other topics of interest, such as the implementation and political economy of the reforms, or the effect of the 1980s crisis on social sectors, are not dealt with here.

Education Sector

The current structure of Chile's education system is based on reforms introduced around 1980.[2] Until that time, the country relied on a centralized system

* The authors are grateful for the valuable cooperation of Olimpia Icochea and Flavia Kuncar in preparing this chapter. They also wish to thank José Angulo for his computer assistance and the many persons interviewed who provided valuable background on the topic. A special thanks goes to Raúl Allard, Undersecretary of Education, for making the data base of SIMCE tests available. The contents and conclusions expressed here are entirely our own.

[1] The general bibliographical references on Chilean social policy used throughout this chapter include Castañeda, 1991; Haindl, Budinich, and Irarrázaval, 1989; MIDEPLAN, 1991b and 1991c; Mujica and Larrañaga, 1992; and The World Bank, 1991 and 1989.

[2] This section is based on bibliographical references that include Castañeda, 1991; The World Bank, 1989 and 1991; Espínola, 1991; Edwards, Assaél and López, 1991; Magendzo, Egaña and Latorre, 1988; Latorre, Núñez, Gonzáles, et al., 1991; Levin, 1991; Henríquez, 1991; and Casassus, 1989.

whereby the Ministry of Education was responsible for funding and providing education, procuring related necessities, and building schools. The system was characterized by inferior quality and high dropout and failure rates. Among the factors that contributed to this situation were lack of incentives for school administrators, low salaries and high administrative costs, inadequate supervision, rigid or inflexible curricula, and little community participation in school-related matters.

The reform tried to reverse this situation first by decentralizing public education and transferring school administration to the municipalities. Second, the private sector was allowed, with some restrictions, to provide education under public funding. Third, a financing mechanism was introduced whereby subsidies were granted on the basis of student enrollment.

Important changes were also made in higher education. The existing system offered little diversity, and the allocation of government funds was not based on performance criteria. Furthermore, universities were not motivated to encourage efficiency and thus grew in an unstructured fashion. In 1981, the system underwent a series of reforms resulting in greater participation by the private sector, the creation of professional institutes and technical training centers, and autonomy for the regional branches of existing traditional universities. Government financial assistance was provided in three ways: direct contributions to fund research and development, indirect contributions to universities enrolling the top 20,000 students, and loans for needy students. These funds provided a valuable financial infusion to the sector.

Education in Chile is currently provided through a mixed system, whereby both the private and public sectors participate in financing and production of education activities. State-subsidized education is decentralized and provided by private and municipal contractors. The role of the Ministry of Education is to supervise and coordinate the sector's activities and to formulate general education policies.

There are four educational levels in Chile: pre-school, elementary, secondary, and higher education. Pre-school attendance is voluntary for children between the ages of two and five. Elementary education lasts for eight years and is compulsory. Secondary education, which is voluntary, offers two program options: science-humanities (four years) or technical-vocational (five years). Higher education is composed of a wide variety of institutions and options.

Nearly all of the resources in pre-school, elementary, and secondary education are concentrated at the elementary level. In 1990, this sector accounted for 68 percent of total student enrollment and 58 percent of all teachers and institutions. The secondary level accounted for 24.5 percent of enrollment, 36 percent of teachers, and 14 percent of institutions. The corresponding figures for the pre-school level were 7.5 percent, 6 percent, and 28 percent, respectively. The student/teacher ratio was 26 or 27 to 1 at the elementary and pre-school levels, and 15.4 to 1 at the secondary level.

Education at the pre-school, elementary, and secondary levels is provided through tuition-supported private schools, subsidized private schools, and municipal schools. Tuition-supported private schools are owned by private individuals or organizations and receive most of their support through tuition fees. On the other hand, subsidized private schools and municipal schools are, in general, tuition-free and rely mainly on state contributions for their support.

In 1990, municipal schools accounted for approximately 60 percent of student enrollment, teachers, and institutions. Subsidized schools followed with about 28 percent of enrollment, teachers, and schools. Private education constitutes a relatively smaller sector.

Higher education is provided through universities, professional institutions, and technical training centers. Of these, only universities can confer academic degrees required for the longer, more academically prestigious disciplines (five or more years). Professional institutes offer nonacademic degree programs that usually last around four to five years. Technical training centers offer short, nonacademic degree programs (two to three years).

Universities are divided into two large groups: institutions funded by the state, which include the country's oldest and most prestigious universities (the so-called traditional universities) and their regional branches, and universities created after 1981, which are virtually unfunded by the government and which usually offer low-cost training programs. These universities generally hire part-time personnel and depend on tuition for their support.

In 1990, there were a total of 60 universities with an enrollment of 132,500 students. Of these, eight were traditional and 14 were regional universities. The remaining 38 belonged to the new group of private institutions that, for their part, accounted for only 15 percent of university enrollment. On the other hand, in 1990 there were 82 professional institutes with approximately 25,000 students, and 156 technical training centers with 55,600 students.

Figure 2.1 illustrates resource flows in education. Fiscal spending represents 56.5 percent of total spending; tuition payments, 31.8 percent; and the remaining 11.7 percent corresponds to other incomes.

In pre-school, elementary, and secondary education, government contributions to the municipal system account for 25 percent of total spending, while contributions to subsidized private schools account for 13.5 percent. Tuition-supported private schools receive around 17.5 percent of the sector's spending through tuition fees.

In higher education, fiscal contributions to traditional and regional universities account for 9.5 percent of the sector's spending, and student government loans account for another 1.6 percent. The remaining institutions in the sector receive minimal government assistance.

Figure 2.1. Resource Flows in the Education Sector
(percent)

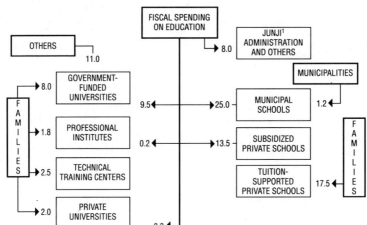

Source: Author's calculations based on sector statistics.
[1] National Board of Pre-school Centers.

Tuition is an important source of funding for higher education. Tuition fees for traditional and regional universities represent 8 percent of total spending on education (26 percent of their budget); for professional institutes, 1.8 percent (90 percent of budget); for private universities, 2 percent (90 percent of budget); and for technical training centers, 2.5 percent (100 percent of budget). Traditional and regional universities also raise an amount equivalent to 11 percent of spending (40 percent of budget) through selling services, grants-in-aid, and other means.

Public resources for pre-school, elementary, and secondary education are allocated as subsidies based on the number of students. These are intended to cover all of the schools' overhead costs, including teacher salaries, educational materials, and building maintenance. This mechanism was designed to encourage competition among schools to attract and maintain high levels of enrollment. This competition, in turn, encourages greater efficiency and quality of services because school incomes depend on student enrollment.

Government funding in higher education is channeled through several mechanisms. Principal among them are direct, unrestricted contributions granted on the basis of long-standing criteria (51 percent of total contributions in 1992); competitive contributions awarded on the basis of student merit and quality of research and development projects (30.5 percent); and different types of student aid, such as loans and scholarships (18.5 percent).

Table 2.1. Chile: Educational Coverage by Income Level, 1990
(percent)

Education	Quintile of per capita family income[1]					Total
	I	II	III	IV	V	
Pre-school	17.0	17.8	21.4	24.4	33.6	21.0
Elementary	95.6	96.2	97.4	98.2	98.2	96.7
Secondary	71.4	79.6	77.8	86.1	96.2	80.2
Higher	7.7	8.5	11.2	18.9	36.3	15.6

Source: MIDEPLAN (1992a).
Note: [1] Quintile I represents the lowest level of income; quintile V, the highest.

Coverage in elementary education—defined as the percentage of children between the ages of 6 and 13 who attend elementary schools—is high and relatively similar among the different income strata (Table 2.1). On the other hand, coverage in secondary education—measured by students between the ages of 14 and 18 who attend secondary schools—amounts to about 60 percent and varies significantly according to family income. This characteristic is even more pronounced at the level of higher education, which covers about 12 percent of young people between the ages of 19 and 24. Coverage at this level varies significantly according to family income.

Figures showing the distribution of public spending (Table 2.2) on pre-school, elementary, and secondary education reflect, on the one hand, the universal coverage of education programs, and, on the other, the process of self-selection undertaken by higher-income families who prefer to send their children to superior and costlier tuition-supported private schools. Moreover, public spending on education is clearly regressive (i.e., diminishing) because of the socioeconomic make-up of university student bodies. In any event, the relatively higher allocations channeled to elementary and secondary education, and the fact that not all allocations to higher education are social spending (research funding), contribute to a progressive structure of social spending (i.e., increases) in the education system as a whole.

General Evaluation of Public Education

By Latin American standards, Chile's population enjoys a high level of education. In 1990, the country's illiteracy rate was 5.4 percent, and the average number of years of schooling for individuals over 15 was 8.33 for men and 9.14 for women. Elementary school coverage is almost universal; secondary school coverage is adequate. However, serious doubts exist concerning the quality and pedagogical soundness of education in Chile. Indeed, improvement of its edu-

Table 2.2. Distribution of Public Spending on Education, 1990
(percent)

Education	Quintile of per capita family income[1]					Total
	I	II	III	IV	V	
Pre-school	27.6	28.8	20.3	13.6	9.7	100.0
Elementary	35.7	26.9	18.1	12.6	6.7	100.0
Secondary (Science and Humanities)	23.5	24.1	21.0	18.1	13.3	100.0
Secondary (Technical and Vocational)	25.8	29.7	22.8	15.9	5.8	100.0
University credit	22.8	15.8	21.8	19.9	19.7	100.0

Source: MIDEPLAN (1993).
Note: [1] Quintile I represents the lowest level of income; quintile V, the highest.

cation system is one of the most important challenges the country faces in the future.

Elementary and secondary state-supported schools offer poor-quality education. National achievement test results for fourth and eighth grade students and college admission test results point to a significant disparity between tuition-supported private schools and state-supported schools (both private and municipal).

According to experts, students who are taught by old-fashioned, rote methods of learning that are unresponsive to their needs suffer from serious problems in comprehension. Yet new teachers continue to be trained in this methodology, thus creating a vicious circle that is difficult to break.

Curricula for secondary education are not well defined. Most high school students receive a general education designed to prepare them for college. In reality, however, few students actually enter universities. Technical-vocational secondary schools prepare young people for the labor market. Preliminary studies, however, question the efficiency of this kind of education. In short, and as one high-level advisor to the Ministry of Education has observed, the structure and content of secondary education as established in 1967 are totally out of step with the country's development.

Efforts to improve the quality of elementary education center on the MECE project (Mejoramiento de la Calidad de la Educación). The purpose of this $240 million project, which is financed by the World Bank, is to improve public education infrastructures, text books, teacher training programs, and other areas.[3] The project also aims at encouraging teachers to become more actively involved in competitive projects that contribute to school development. However, the

---

[3] Amounts are in U.S. dollars unless otherwise indicated.

MECE project does not provide economic incentives for teachers. This may be one of the project's major drawbacks, given the current low status of teacher salaries. Moreover, the project provides for only temporary, rather than incremental, or permanent assistance.

The issue of quality in education is linked to financing. Public spending on education is low, whether measured by teacher salaries or compared with spending on private education. However, the enormous size of the public system, which accounts for over 90 percent of elementary and secondary enrollments, makes it difficult to fund improvements solely through fiscal contributions. This questions the validity of not relying on direct contributions from users. A system that, because of insufficient funds, provides an inferior product to individuals willing to pay for something better, is clearly ineffective. Although several attempts have been made to remedy this situation, the prevailing position of the Ministry of Education and its related agencies has been to avoid changes.

Furthermore, the sector's authorities have been unwilling to make national achievement scores and college admission test results available. This practice is incompatible with a competitive system that provides direct subsidies based on student enrollment. In such a system, parents need access to all available information in order to make decisions.

The institutional culture of the sector opposes any type of "intrusion" by other professionals in matters related to educational policy. However, the complexity and externalities of the system require input from specialists in areas outside of education. Thus, economics of education, an area well-established in developed countries, has found virtually no place in Chile's education system.

Two especially vulnerable areas exist in higher education. First, the issue of public funding—still a matter of open debate—concerns levels of fiscal contribution to higher education, targets for such contributions (research, students, etc.), funding mechanisms (fixed contributions or contributions based on achievement), and the relationship between fiscal contributions and cost containment. The second issue relates to government regulation of the sector's institutions. The emergence of many new institutions over the past few years has raised reasonable doubts concerning program quality and oversupplies produced in certain professional areas.

The Health Sector

The current structure of Chile's health system began to take shape at the end of the 1970s.[4] Until that time, the country relied on a centralized public health sec-

---

[4] This section is based on a set of bibliographical references including the Ministry of Health, 1992a, 1992b, and 1992c; and Miranda, 1990.

tor whereby the National Health Service was the main provider of in-patient and out-patient care. Under this system, beneficiaries were not free to choose their own health care provider or insurance program.

Substantive changes to the system were introduced beginning in 1979. These resulted in the Ministry of Health limiting its activities to coordinating and formulating health policies. The public system was decentralized through the creation of the Office of Health Services and the transfer of primary health care centers to the municipalities. Allocation criteria attempting to link financing to performance were incorporated in the public system, and private health insurance companies were created.

Chile has a mixed health system in which both the private and public sectors participate in insurance, financing, and health service delivery (Figure 2.2).

The Ministry of Health is responsible for formulating policies and programs, coordinating the sector's organizations, and supervising, evaluating, and controlling health policies. The system consists of 26 autonomous health services that oversee a hospital infrastructure of 188 facilities. These hospitals provide different types of secondary and tertiary health care, including specialized medical services, emergency treatment, dental care, laboratory testing, imaging procedures, surgery, and childbirth services. Primary health care is provided by 329 clinics and 996 centers. Most of these facilities are operated by the municipality of the respective region. Primary care clinics are responsible for child health care (from the neo-natal stage until the age of 14), disease control, adult and adolescent health care, pregnancy care, and family planning. The public sector's financing agency is the National Health Fund (FONASA), a decentralized service responsible for collecting, managing, and allocating financial resources to the sector.

The private health system comprises health insurance companies (ISAPRE) and private health care providers. The Superintendency of ISAPRE, a decentralized public agency, registers and oversees the operation of these organizations. It is also responsible for registering and funding these organizations.

Active and retired workers are required to contribute 7 percent of their gross income to the health system. Payment is forwarded either to FONASA, if the individual is enrolled in the public system, or to one of the ISAPRE companies, if he or she subscribes to a private health plan. ISAPRE subscribers are required to pay a minimum contribution, which may amount to more than 7 percent of their income.

The structure of the health insurance and medical service system is illustrated in Figure 2.3, which shows that subscribers who pay premiums belong to FONASA or to an ISAPRE company. On the other hand, the poor, or those who do not pay premiums, belong to FONASA and are given special treatment. FONASA subscribers can choose between two options: institutional coverage or a free choice plan. Those who choose institutional coverage are cared for in public health facilities: hospitals and primary care centers. Hospital care is sub-

Figure 2.2. Structure of Health Sector

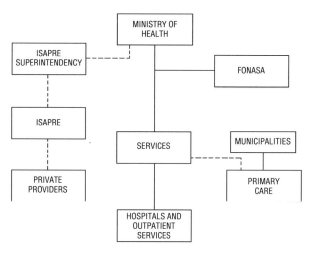

Source: Prepared by author.

ject to a co-payment based on patient income levels. Treatment in primary care centers, on the other hand, does not require a co-payment. Subscribers to the free choice plan receive care from participating private health care providers and pay fees set by the providers and not necessarily based on income levels. Under this scheme, the population is divided into three groups. The first two comprise individuals whose incomes fall below a certain level and those who are enrolled in government assistance programs. These groups are exempt from co-payments. The rest of the population pays 25 percent or 50 percent of the service fee, depending on their level of income. Non-premium-paying beneficiaries of the public system cannot subscribe to the free choice plan. On the other hand, ISAPRE subscribers receive care from private health care providers and are subject to co-payments as stipulated in their insurance contracts. Co-payments vary according to premium rates, the number of dependents, and the amount of coverage provided.

The public system accounts for 53.5 percent of total spending on health (Figure 2.4). Main revenue sources include premium payments by FONASA's subscribers (27 percent of total spending) and fiscal contributions from the country's budget (18 percent of the total). A third source of income for the public system, which amounts to 8.5 percent of health-related spending, is the co-payment plan for free choice care and for institutional services. FONASA receives the fiscal allocations and premiums to transfer them to health services and private care

Figure 2.3. Structure of Health Insurance System and Medical Services

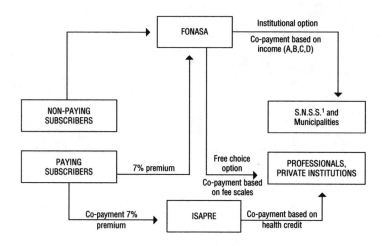

Source: Miranda (1990).
[1] National Health Services System.

providers participating in the free choice system. The health services, in turn, transfer the funds to public hospitals (37 percent) and primary care centers (7.5 percent), and provide various subsidies (2 percent) as payments for medical licenses and for maternity services (not shown in the diagram). In 1990, ISAPRE companies received premiums amounting to 39 percent of spending on health and co-payments equal to 6.5 percent. Part of these resources were retained in the ISAPRE system either as remittances for services and administrative expenses or as profits. The ISAPRE system transferred 35 percent of the resources to private providers.

Hospitals receive their financing in two main ways: wages and salaries, and a mechanism of billing for services rendered (FAP). The FAP is used to finance just the purchase of supplies. Primary care centers receive all of their funding—for both supplies and salaries—through a mechanism of billing for services rendered at municipal centers (FAPEM). Municipalities supplement the FAPEM contributions.

Wage and salary rates for the nearly 60,000 hospital employees are based on type of employment and are governed by a common salary scale. The scale fixes salary levels according to the employee's professional qualifications, experience, and place of employment. The Ministry of Finance sets staffing levels for hospitals within budget allocations.

The FAP is a cost-recovery system based on the amount of the billed services. Every health care service billed at more than Ch$2,200 includes a charge

Figure 2.4. Financial Flow Chart of Health Sector, 1990[1]

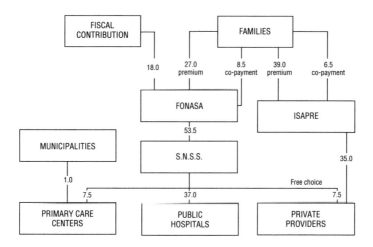

Source: Author's calculations based on sector statistics.
[1] Excludes private spending outside the ISAPRE system, and public spending on nutrition and investment programs.

for service and staff overhead. This is defined as gross FAP. Each month, FONASA reimburses health care providers the cost incurred in supplying products and services in accordance with billings evaluated as net FAP (a fraction of gross costs after substracting staff salaries).

In 1990, about 70 percent of the population was covered by public insurance (Table 2.3), while public coverage for poor families in the lower two income quintiles exceeded 80 percent. ISAPRE companies provided coverage for 15 percent of the population, with a significant concentration on high-income quintiles.[5] The group identified in Table 2.3 as "private"—accounting for about 12 percent of the population—represents individuals not covered by either the public or private systems. Part of this group, however, still depends on the public system since, when in need, they receive health care from public hospitals.

Data on coverage and financial resources show that per capita outlays in the public system amount to 22 percent of those in the ISAPRE system. This figure illustrates the split within the health insurance system, where the public sector component serves mostly medium- and low-income individuals, while ISAPRE tends to serve the high-income sector. The difference in per capita

---

[5] This section is based on a set of bibliographical references including the Ministry of Health, 1992a, 1992b, and 1992c; and Miranda, 1990.

Table 2.3. Health System Coverage by Income Level in Chile, 1990
(percent)

Income quintile[1]	Public system	ISAPRE	Private	Others	Total
I	84.5	2.5	10.3	2.6	100.0
II	80.5	5.4	11.1	3.0	100.0
III	71.3	11.1	13.7	3.9	100.0
IV	58.6	22.3	13.4	5.7	100.0
V	37.2	44.0	12.7	6.1	100.0
Total[2]	68.7	15.1	12.1	4.1	100.0
	(8,746)	(1,922)	(1,543)	(515)	(12,909)

Source: MIDEPLAN (1992d).
Notes: [1] Quintile I represents the lowest level of income; quintile V, the highest.
[2] Total population (in thousands) shown in parentheses.

spending suggests, moreover, that the quality of the two services is significantly different.

The distribution of health care programs is shown in the first line of Table 2.4. Around 52 percent of public health care outlays go to families belonging to the poorer 40 percent of the population. About 9 percent of the outlays go to families in the high-income quintile. The tables reflect the universal coverage provided by the public system and the self-exclusion of high-income sectors. The second line in Table 2.4 shows the distribution of contributions to the system. The distribution is progressive, reflecting beneficiary income levels and the relationship between premiums and co-payments. The net effect of health care outlays is shown in the last line of the table. In the public system, high-income subscribers subsidize low-income subscribers. In 1990, this subsidy amounted to $65.2 million. Benefits paid to middle-income subscribers (fourth quintile) are almost equal to the amount of their contributions.

Evaluation of the Public Health Care System

Based on the level of health indicators, Chile's public health care system has achieved excellent results. The country's infant mortality and life expectancy rates are similar to those of developed countries, proof that the health care system is very effective. Contributing factors include an appropriate targeting policy that emphasizes preventive health, highly trained staffs, appropriate environmental health measures, and a highly educated population.

A health policy emphasizing primary health care allowed the country to combat infectious diseases successfully. Other aspects of health care, however, have been neglected. The country's current epidemiological profile, which is

Table 2.4. Statistics of Health Care Programs in Chile, 1990

	Income quintile[1]				
	I	II	III	IV	V
Distribution of	27.5[2]	24.7	22.1	16.9	8.8
spending	128.1[3]	115.4	103.0	79.0	41.1
Distribution of	5.0[2]	13.5	20.3	25.6	35.6
contributions	14.8[3]	40.3	59.5	76.4	106.3
Net effect	113.3[3]	75.1	43.5	2.6	(65.2)

Source: MIDEPLAN (1993).

Notes: [1] Quintile I represents the lowest level of income; quintile V, the highest.

   [2] Figures in top row are percentages.

   [3] Figures in bottom row are in millions of U.S. dollars.

characterized by chronic noninfectious diseases, suggests a need to reevaluate and adjust the system.

An enormous gap now exists between the private and public health systems. High- and middle-income individuals enrolled in the private system rely on timely health care and access to modern facilities and technologies. Yet, most of the population is covered under the public system and has to cope with deteriorating facilities, long waiting lines, and generally inadequate treatment. These shortcomings—particularly deteriorated hospital facilities and low staff salaries—are in part the result of the 1980 reduction in fiscal allocations.

Decentralization, which was introduced over a decade ago, has not yielded the expected results. The Ministry of Health still controls health services, even in those areas in which autonomy has been granted. Allocation of resources within the system is, in practice, based on past criteria—not on the achievement and efficiency criteria proposed by the reform in the 1980s. Three main reasons underlie these shortcomings. First, significant workforce-related constraints limited the effect of decentralization. Health care workers and hospital personnel are civil servants. This complicates salary and contract policy adjustments. Hospital and health service administrators thus are severely limited in providing economic incentives that would increase the sector's efficiency and quality and are not free to make needed personnel changes. The municipally operated primary care sector has had greater flexibility in this regard since all the sector's employees receive equal treatment. This situation may be changed if a new law intending to eliminate such flexibility—the municipal health worker's statute—is enacted. This statute, a response to pressure from the labor unions, is being justified on the grounds that it provides workers with job security as a way of compensating for low salaries.

Second, the programs that allocate FAP and FAPEM resources have not fulfilled their goals because of the tension between capped budgets and cost-recovery schemes based on delivered services. Clearly, there is no reason why these two variables should reconcile. The meaning of the FAP and FAPEM mechanism has been lost because past financial straits have made budgetary restraint the relevant consideration. The problem, however, goes beyond financial matters and is ultimately linked to the issue of cost containment.

Third, decentralization proved to be a difficult task because of administrative problems and a lack of human resources in the public health system. The management of health care services and hospitals is primarily in the hands of individuals who lack expertise in managing human and financial resources. This has created problems in institutional management and development, problems that have been classified as "dramatic" in a recent evaluation of the system. The general level of incompetence has also stood in the way of health services and hospitals in taking full advantage of the autonomy granted by the reform.

Two important considerations are worth noting in the level and structure of health resources. First, the revenue structure of the public health system is basically adequate. As previously described, this structure is based on a combination of fiscal contributions, premiums, and direct charges. Accordingly, subscribers contribute directly to the system in proportion to their income level. The contribution is supplemented by a co-payment at the time the health care service is supplied. Only the co-payment mechanism needs improving by appropriately registering and billing subscribers. This control is necessary because a reconciliation of cost-recovery estimates with the income distribution of the system's subscribers reveals that cheating is prevalent. Second, the system requires greater financial support. The hospital infrastructure, health-related acquisitions, and personnel salaries have deteriorated, as evidenced by the exodus of trained personnel to the private sector or to other professional fields. This trend has been enhanced by the creation of the ISAPRE companies and by the competition for human resources they engender. The sector's organizational shortcomings show, therefore, a need for reforms. These reforms should precede any allocation of new resources to ensure their appropriate use.

The equity of the public system can be evaluated in two ways. If one compares the public and private health systems, the cited disparity in resources and quality emerges. This, for many critics of ISAPRE, is proof of that system's evils. One basis for the criticism is that current ISAPRE premium payers were former FONASA contributors who helped finance the public system through subsidy transfers. When these contributors moved to ISAPRE plans, public system revenues declined. However, the decline should be offset by greater fiscal infusions since health beneficiaries should not be responsible for subsidizing services to the poorer ones.

The internal equity of the public health system is also questionable. While the emphasis on fully subsidizing those of lesser means is generally correct, there are, however, two areas of concern. First, a public system whereby high-income beneficiaries subsidize low-income individuals is unstable and inefficient. Subsidy transfers introduce instabilities in the system because they clearly induce high-income beneficiaries to switch to a private system that provides additional and superior services. Indeed, this predicament has characterized the health care system since ISAPRE was created in 1981. The migration of high-income subscribers from the public to the private system has contributed to the financial drain of the former. The drain has provoked remedial public measures, such as the premium increase from 4 percent in the early 1980s to the current 7 percent, raising criticism about the cohesiveness of the health system. However, it is desirable to use the public financing to pursue redistributive goals; otherwise, unnecessary distortions in the allocation of health care resources are introduced.

Finally, it should be pointed out that a series of initiatives are being studied and implemented to overcome the described shortcomings of the public health system. Highlighted among these are a significant program of investments in infrastructure and technological modernization; a reform aimed at substituting a prospective diagnosis payment system for the FAP system and a prospective per capita payment system for the FAPEM; an in-depth study on different service-related costs; and a human resource policy based on training, salary adjustments, and improved managerial professionalism.

Financial Subsidies and Food Programs

Financial Subsidies

Financial subsidies are cash contributions that the state provides to poorer families.[6] They are intended to provide assistance in the form of income to those who are most needy and cannot work. The major programs include family allowances, assistance pensions, and single family subsidies (See Table 2.5).

Family allowance is a subsidy for family dependents belonging to a formal insurance program. The subsidy is granted to children under the age of 18 (or unmarried students under 24), all handicapped dependents (regardless of age), unemployed spouses, widowed mothers, orphans, and seniors over 65.

Although family allowance is an important state financial assistance program, its universal character makes it costly and inefficient. For this reason, in 1990 family allowance was divided into three levels based on income, thus improving the targeting and efficiency of the subsidy.

---

6 This section is based on a set of bibliographical references that include MIDEPLAN, 1991d, 1992b, and 1992c; Raczynski, 1991; and Torche, 1985 and 1990.

Table 2.5. Financial Subsidies to Chile's Poorest Families, 1990

Financial subsidy	Social spending percentage	Benefit[1]	Beneficiaries[2]	Access requirement
Family				Social insurance
Allowance	7.5	1.8-5.1	3,735	system registration
SUF	2.0	5.1	679	CAS record[3], age
PASIS [4]	8.0	26.5	311	CAS record[3], age

Source: MIDEPLAN (1992a).
Notes: [1] Monthly allowance in Chilean pesos.
[2] In thousands.
[3] Record providing socioeconomic characteristics.
[4] Assistance pensions.

The purpose of the single family subsidy (SUF) is to provide assistance to people with limited resources and no access to insurance programs. The program targets parents or guardians of children under the age of 15 and pregnant women in extreme poverty.

The SUF subsidy is provided by municipalities based on information provided in what is known as the CAS-2 record. This record provides the means for identifying the extremely poor and for channeling assistance programs to the neediest segments of the population. Several requirements must be fulfilled in order to qualify for the subsidy. Children under the age of six must participate in a control program established by the Ministry of Health, and those over the age of six need to show proof of enrollment in a school facility. The SUF program lasts for three years and is renewable for another three, as long as requirements are met. However, not everyone who is eligible receives SUF benefits because of limits in the number of subsidies that can be granted. According to estimates, SUF covers only 51.2 percent of the eligible population.

Assistance pensions (PASIS) are forms of financial aid to those over 65, uninsured handicapped individuals over 18, and those whose monthly per capita incomes do not exceed 50 percent of the minimum pension payment. As in the case of the SUF, the enrollment and selection of beneficiaries by the municipalities is based on information provided in the CAS-2 record. PASIS's benefits expire when the beneficiary dies or when the pension is not collected for six consecutive months. According to available estimates, PASIS covers only 51.9 percent of eligible seniors because of limits in the number of PASIS's pensions that can be granted.

Preference for financial subsidies is given to the population's poorest households (Table 2.6). Poor households—that is, those belonging to the first two income quintiles—received around 80 percent of the financial subsidies granted in 1990 by the PASIS and SUF assistance programs.

Table 2.6. Distribution of Financial Subsidies in Chile, 1990
(percent)

	Quintile[1]					Total
	I	II	III	IV	V	
Family Allowance	21.6	25.7	21.2	17.6	13.9	100.0
SUF	50.7	29.3	13.6	4.8	1.5	100.0
PASIS	45.5	22.2	19.4	10.0	2.9	100.0

Source: MIDEPLAN (1992a).
Note: [1]Quintile I represents the lowest level of income; quintile V, the highest.

Table 2.7. Financial Subsidies as a Percent of Autonomous Income in Chile, 1990

Income Decile[1]	Individual Income	Family Allowance	PASIS Subsidies	SUF Subsidies	Other	Total
I	100	5.8	7.0	4.9	5.4	23.0
II	100	5.0	1.3	1.4	0.2	7.9
III	100	3.3	0.9	0.8	0.4	5.3
IV	100	2.4	0.4	0.5	0.3	3.4
V	100	1.8	0.4	0.2	0.1	2.6
VI	100	1.3	0.3	0.2	0.1	1.8
VII	100	1.0	0.2	0.1	0.0	1.3
VIII	100	0.7	0.1	0.0	0.0	0.9
IX	100	0.4	0.0	0.0	0.0	0.5
X	100	0.2	0.0	0.0	0.0	0.2
Total	100	0.9	0.2	0.2	0.2	1.4

Source: MIDEPLAN (1992a).
Note: [1]Decile I represents the lowest income; decile X, the highest.

Financial subsidies represent a significant part of poor families' incomes. (Table 2.7). In 1990, financial subsidies raised income levels of the poorest decile by 23 percent. Respective increases for the second and third deciles were 7.9 percent and 5.3 percent, respectively. The cited subsidies represent marginal income increases for the less-impoverished, as a result of targeting mechanisms and insignificant benefit amounts.

Food Programs

State assistance for nutrition targets the segment of Chile's population classified as biologically vulnerable, that is, those segments that require greater nutritional assistance and are, therefore, most likely to suffer caloric deficiencies. Therefore, nutritional assistance programs target children under the age of six, pregnant women, nursing mothers, and elementary school children. Currently, social nutritional outlays are concentrated in two programs: National Program for Supplementary Nutrition (PNAC) and the School Lunch Program (PAE).

The PNAC has been in operation for more than 20 years. Its purpose is to improve the health of pregnant women and of children under the age of six. A specific objective of the program is to prevent and reverse infant malnutrition through the delivery of dairy products, rice, and heavy soups. A requirement for receiving food is to have regular health check-ups in primary care SNSS (National System of Health Services) centers and municipal facilities. This program allows for the monitoring of child development, the prevention of ill-nesses, and the implementation of immunization and hygiene-awareness programs. Coverage is universal. Children under the age of six, pregnant women, and nursing mothers who fulfill the requirement for periodic health checks are entitled to receive benefits.

PNAC comprises two subprograms: the basic program that is applied to young children, pregnant women, and nursing mothers in normal nutritional situations and the reinforcement program that benefits people at risk. PNAC's nutritional contribution, expressed in calories and protein, declines with the age of the child. Food in the basic program covers, on the average, 50 percent of the daily caloric needs and 170 percent of protein needs during the first year of life. Calories and protein content decline to 14 percent and 43 percent respectively in the one-to-two age group, and to 10 percent and 33 percent for pre-schoolers.

The administration and financing of PNAC is decentralized, with annual budgets allocated to each health service based on the number of people in the program. The Ministry of Health has a regulatory role in so far as it supervises and evaluates the success of program objectives. The PNAC accounts for around 10 percent of public outlays on health. The main factors used for determining PNAC outlays are the number and kind of beneficiaries, the price fluctuations of the products distributed, and the Ministry of Health's budget constraints.

The PAE consists of daily delivery of food rations to 6-to-14 year old children who are enrolled in publicly funded elementary schools. The program was created in 1964 to reduce failure, dropout, and school absentee rates, as well as improve student performance. In its current version, the program emphasizes nutritional and educational objectives. The PAE consists of three types of food programs: food rations containing 700 calories and 20 grams of protein (33 percent of the FAO-OMS recommendations), reinforcement rations of 1,000 calories and 30 grams of protein (40 percent), and breakfast and snack rations of 350 calories for rural school children.

The program is directed and funded by a National Board for School Aid and Scholarships (JUNAEB), an entity dependent on the Ministry of Education. The board's budget currently represents about 8 percent of ministry outlays. All of

Table 2.8. Distribution of Food Programs in Chile, 1990
(percent)

	Income quintile[1]					Total
	I	II	III	IV	V	
PAE	52.4	27.3	13.2	5.3	1.8	100.0
PNAC	38.0	30.9	18.1	9.5	3.5	100.0

Source: MIDEPLAN (1993).
Note: [1]Quintile I represents the lowest level of income; quintile V, the highest.

the food services are contracted to private concessions. For this purpose, public biddings are held every three years, with selection based on price and quality.

Despite the program's universal coverage, food delivery in PNAC's primary care health control centers results in targeting through self-selection. PNAC coverage in 1990 was about 90 percent and 85 percent for the first and second income quintiles, respectively (Table 2.8).

PAE targeting has undergone several changes over time. Today, targeting methods are based on forecast models that select variables dependent on food insufficiencies. Ration allocation is based on the following criteria: rations of 1,000 calories are assigned to schools whose students have the greatest nutritional needs, and schools with average needs receive rations of 700 calories. In each school, the teachers are responsible for distributing the food to students. Schools whose students have low nutritional needs do not receive help.

Evaluation of Financial Subsidy and Food Programs

Chile has been relatively successful with its financial subsidy programs. The goal of the SUF and PASIS assistance has been to channel resources to the neediest individuals and to those whose age or physical condition prevent them from working. The CAS-2 record allows careful targeting of the subsidies.

Given the small amount of benefits available to individuals, the subsidies supplement rather than replace family income. The lack of incentives characteristic of assistance programs is therefore not a problem. Those capable of working do not receive subsidies.

The targeting process used in the family allowance program has transformed it into an efficient vehicle for helping low-income families who are enrolled in pension plans. This has resulted, however, in a reduction of the marginal benefits for high-income individuals. If the benefits received by the wealthiest quintile were transferred to the lowest-income quintile, incomes for the latter would increase by nearly 6 percent, while incomes for the wealthiest quintile would decrease by about 0.3 percent. This example illustrates the rational nature of the targeting process. More importantly, it shows the inefficiency of blanket subsidies that are intended as price controls on certain products of mass consumption.

Food programs are part of a nutritional policy that was highly effective in reducing infant malnutrition and that achieved its objective some time ago. This is particularly true in the case of the PNAC, a program with more explicit nutritional objectives than those of the PAE, which emphasized educational goals. In any case, from a strictly nutritional standpoint, a question arises whether these programs have conformed to the country's nutritional profile. The most recent PNAC evaluations took place in 1979; the next one will take place in 1993. The results of the upcoming study will be crucial in deciding the future of the program.

A central theme for both food programs is their interrelationship with other social programs: health check-ups in the case of the PNAC and school attendance in the case of PAE. It has been observed that physical check-ups are very important and that demand for PNAC food assistance is related to health check-ups. Thus, the need for food assistance declines as the child gets older and as the intervals between check-ups increase, suggesting a need for revision of the program's structure and objectives.

On the other hand, the PAE's main objective is to encourage school attendance and to make delivery of pedagogical materials more efficient. There is evidence that a correlation exists between the PAE and class attendance. However, no reference exists on the effect of PAE on school performance.

In short, both programs have fulfilled an important task but need to be constantly evaluated to decide whether they should continue in their present form, or whether changes need to be introduced to improve performance.

Quality and Demand in Elementary Education

This section presents an empirical analysis of quality and demand in Chile's schools. The study was carried out in the metropolitan areas of Chile, which account for about 36 percent of national enrollment. Data constraints make it necessary to deal with the topics separately, even though the interdependence between demand decisions and quality of schools would make a simultaneous analysis preferable.

Of great interest is a comparison between municipal and subsidized private schools, which receive equal subsidies for each student. Differences between the demand or quality of the schools would identify the eventual advantages of one institution over the other.

The information comes from two data bases. The Ministry of Education provided the results of the tests measuring quality standards in education (SIMCE) for 1990 and 1991. This data contains achievement test scores of

Table 2.9. School Statistics by Type, 1990-91[1]
(percent)

	Municipal School	Subsidized Private School	Paid Private School
Promotion rate	89.51	90.50	95.00
Failure rate	7.58	6.19	2.36
Dropout rate	2.90	3.31	2.65
Spanish SIMCE, 4th grade	56.28	62.30	79.31
Mathematics SIMCE, 4th grade	54.65	60.61	78.76
Spanish SIMCE, 8th grade	49.53	53.91	69.84
Mathematics SIMCE, 8th grade	44.92	48.34	68.60
Students per course	32.75	34.80	25.29
No. of teachers	14.66	10.32	11.44
Schools in poor communities[2]	65.60	60.50	9.70

Notes. [1]Except for the information on the SIMCE for the eighth grade, all the figures shown are for 1990.
[2]Those where the poor comprise 30 percent or more of the population.

fourth and eighth grade students in mathematics and Spanish. These scores are used as a proxy to reflect the quality of each institution. Other information taken into account for each school is enrollment, number of courses, personnel, and number of students who passed, failed, and withdrew for each elementary year. The second data base used was the 1990 socioeconomic profile survey (CASEN) that provides information on the socioeconomic background of families.

Quality of Elementary Education

The SIMCE scores for Spanish and mathematics were used as a dependent variable in the equation expressing the quality of the schools. Explanatory variables introduced in the equation were the main inputs used by the schools (number of teachers, school personnel, and number of students per course), the socioeconomic level of the students, as well as the characteristics and institutional affiliation of the schools. Based on information from the 1990 CASEN survey, specific demographic and economic data were obtained on households with children attending elementary schools. Ideally, information on the student body of each school should have been used. However, because that information was not available, common averages by type of school had to be used as substitute indicators for the socioeconomic characteristics of the students of each school. Tables 2.9 and 2.10 present the indicators for the variables considered.

The SIMCE test scores show significant differences among institutional affiliations. Fourth grade students in municipal schools completed only half of

Table 2.10. Household Demographic and Economic Statistics by Type of School (Metropolitan Areas of Chile), 1990

	Average	Standard Deviation
Municipal Schools		
Age of child	10.28	2.66
Age of head of household	45.68	15.31
No. of children (greater than) 6 years	0.58	0.80
No. of children between 6 and 17	2.31	1.15
Household income (U.S. dollars)	332	476
Subsidized Private Schools		
Age of child	9.95	2.53
Age of head of household	47.08	15.30
No. of children (greater than) 6 years	0.57	0.71
No. of children between 6 and 17	2.03	0.96
Household income (U.S. dollars)	448	682
Tuition-Supported Private Schools		
Age of child	9.61	2.54
Age of head of household	50.79	15.40
No. of children (greater than) 6 years	0.47	0.63
No. of children between 6 and 17	2.07	0.88
Household income (U.S. dollars)	1,653	1,287

Source: Authors' calculations based on CASEN 1990.

the minimum objectives required for each grade subject, while children in tuition-supported private schools completed nearly 80 percent of the objectives. The results of students in subsidized private schools exceed those of their municipal counterparts, but are much lower than those in tuition-supported private schools. These differences can also be observed in the eighth grade results. Furthermore, completion of objectives in this grade is significantly lower than that attained in the fourth grade in all of the schools.

Following is the education quality equation used in the econometric analysis of fourth and eighth grade courses in Spanish and mathematics:

$$LnPs_{ij} = F(Ratio_i, Pdoc_i, Padm_i, Aeducy_i, Ingtot_i, Indpob_i, Deps_i, \\ Depp_i, Taprob_{ij}, Trprob_{ij}) \tag{1}$$

where:

F Indicates the linear relationship between the variables in parentheses and the dependent variable.

$LnPs_{ij}$ Is the logarithm of the SIMCE score corresponding to either Spanish (spa) or mathematics (math) for school i and course j.

$Ratio_i$ Is the number of students per course in school i.
$Pdoc_i$ Is the number of professional personnel in school i.
$Padm_i$ Is the number of administrative personnel in school i.
$Aeducy_i$ Indicates the average number of years of schooling for mothers of students attending school i.
$Ingtot_i$ Represents the average total family income of students attending school i.
$Indpob_i$ Is the poverty index for the community where school i is located.
$Desp_i$ Is a variable that takes the value of 1 if i is a subsidized private school.
$Detp_i$ Is a variable that takes the value of 1 if i is a tuition-supported private school.
$Taprob_{ij}$ Indicates the student promotion rate in i school for course j.v
$Trprob_{ij}$ Indicates the student failure rate in i school for course j.

Table 2.11 presents a summary of the impact of the variables used in the four calculations. The detail of the econometric results is presented in the chapter's statistical appendix. Both impact and corresponding elasticities were estimated. The variables that have greater impact in the Spanish and mathematics SIMCE tests for the fourth grade are those that measure school management, such as the student promotion rates, the school's administrative dependency (tuition-supported private and subsidized private), the mother's level of education, and the number of students per course. It can be noted that a 1 percent change in the student promotion rate corresponds to a 0.6 percent increase in the SIMCE Spanish score; a change in the school's affiliation from municipal to tuition-supported private represents a 0.27 percent increase in the SIMCE mathematics score; an additional year of schooling for the mother corresponds to a change of more than 0.1 percent in the performance of her children in Spanish.

The corresponding estimates for the eighth grade confirm the results above. The student promotion rate continues being a fundamental variable in SIMCE performance, as does school affiliation. It should be pointed out that while total family income represents a significant variable in mathematics achievement, its elasticity is quite low: an increase of 1 percent in the total family income implies an increase of 0.03 percent in scholastic achievement.

The effectiveness of the educational system is shown by the fact that the student promotion rate has a positive effect on the SIMCE and that the failure rate has a negative effect. Therefore, the promotion and failure policy in schools is consistent with learning. The SIMCE Spanish score in the fourth grade confirmed that, everything else being constant, subsidized private schools present better student performance than municipal schools. However, the difference between the *Depp* and *Deps* variables indicates that student performance is better in tuition-supported private schools. One conclusion that

Table 2.11. Estimates of Incremental and Elasticity Effects

| | SIMCE scores for 4th grade | | | |
| | Spanish | | Mathematics | |
Variables	Incremental Effect[1]	Decremental Elasticity[2]	Effect[1]	Elasticity[2]
Ratio	0.20	0.11	018	0.10
Pdoc	0.10	0.03	0.12	0.03
Padm	0.25*	0.01*	0.34*	0.01*
Aeducy	0.78	0.11	0.99	0.15
Indpob	-0.35	-0.04	-0.28	-0.04
Deps	5.18	0.09	5.58	0.09
Depp	15.33	0.25	15.91	0.27
Taprob4	37.10	0.57	30.10	0.47
Trprob4	-12,45*	-0.01*	-16.83	-0.02

| | SIMCE scores for 8th grade | | | |
| | Spanish | | Mathematics | |
Variables	Incremental Effect[1]	Decremental Elasticity[2]	Effect[1]	Elasticity[2]
Ratio	0.25	0.16	0.19	0.14
Pdoc	0.17	0.05	0.14	0.05
Indpob/Indpob	0.74	0.12	-0.40	-0.06
Indpob/Totalh	-0.29	-0.04	0.01	0.03
Deps	4.77	0.09	3.93	0.08
Depp	17.53	0.33	19.30	0.40
Trprob8	10.91	0.19	14.24	0.27

Source: Authors' calculations.
Notes: [1] Change in the dependent variable when the corresponding explanatory variable is incremented by one.
[2] Percent change in the dependent variable when the corresponding independent variable is incremented by one percent.
* Insignificant parameter.

can be drawn is that student performance is influenced more by type of affiliation than by variables related to student socioeconomic levels and school characteristics.

Demand for Elementary Education

The following section presents an economic model used to explain the decisions families make regarding different types of elementary schools: municipal, subsidized private, and tuition-supported private. Specifically, the model estimates the effect that the child's socioeconomic and characteristic variables have on the

Table 2.12. Descriptive Statistics of the Models Variables

	Average	Standard deviation	Minimum value	Maximum value
TOTALH	169.35	247.16	0	0.4082E+7
ESCJEFH	9.26	4.38	0	19
EXIAEDUC	7.57	4.63	0	19
DEXISPJA	0.87	0.34	0	1
CNTMN17	2.72	1.26	1	10
SEXO	0.52	0.50	0	1
SEXOJH	0.87	0.34	0	1
DOCUPJH	0.84	0.37	0	1
DINACJH	0.12	0.33	0	1
DWCJH	0.29	0.45	0	1
DZ	0.96	0.20	0	1
DESTADO	0.70	0.46	0	1

Source: Authors' calculations.

probability that a family will opt for a particular type of school. It adopts a methodological framework according to which families select those types of schools that maximize the utility function for the family. To this end, the model discards school nonattendance considerations, given that overall coverage in elementary education in Chile is around 96.7 percent and 97.8 percent at the urban level.

Information from the 1990 CASEN survey was used to evaluate the proposed economic model econometrically. A sample was drawn from students in the metropolitan region who ranged from 6 to 14 years of age and who were attending elementary school at the time of the survey. The dependent variable is of the unordered category type, and each school grade is a category. Among the explanatory variables that were used are total family income *(TOTALH)*; parents' level of education measured as number of years of schooling for head of household *(ESCJEFH)* and of spouse or live-in companion, when one exists *(EXIEDUC)*; the presence of a two-parent household *(DEXISPJA)*, a variable that takes the value of 1 if such a condition exists; the number of school-age siblings *(CNTMN17)*, considered here as the number of children under 17; the sex of the minor *(SEXO)* and of the head of the household *(SEXOJH)*, variables that take the value of 1 for males; a dummy variable for head of household occupation *(DOCUPJH)*; a dummy variable for unemployed status of head of household *(DINACJH)*; a dummy variable for blue collar status of head of household *(WCJH)*; placement of the household in an urban or rural area *(DZ)*, a variable that takes the value of 1 for urban households; and finally, a variable that denotes the health of the minors *(DESTADO)*, that takes the value of 1 if the minor has been sick in the three months before the survey.[7] Descriptive statistics for these variables are presented in Table 2.12.

The econometric methodology uses the Logit Multinomial model whose general formula is:

$$Prob[Y_i = j] = \frac{\exp(ß'_j x_i) j}{\Sigma_j \exp(ß'_j x_i)} = 0, 1 \ldots, J \qquad (2)$$

where $Prob[Y_i = j]$ denotes the probability that the individual or family i chooses alternative j, $j = 0,1, \ldots, J$. To identify the parameters of the model the following normalization was made:

$$ß_0 = 0$$

Table 2.13 shows the main econometric results achieved. (See Tables 2.14–2.17 for additional econometric results). It can be seen that because of the imposed normalization, the only estimated parameters given are for the subsidized and tuition-supported private schools. In general, the independent variables are significant to 5 percent and their estimated impact on the dependent variables is as expected.

The *CNTMN17* variable exhibits a negative sign, which suggests that, all else being constant, an increase in the number of school-age children within the family reduces the probability that the family will send their children to either subsidized or tuition-supported private schools. This is consistent with a lower ability to finance educational expenses per capita in families that have a greater number of school-age children.

The *TOTALH* variable exhibits a positive sign, which suggests that, all else being constant, an increase in family income increases the probability that the children will attend a subsidized or tuition-supported private school. This result is consistent with the greater financial means that higher-income households have for financing a private education.

The level of education of the head of the household *(ESCJEFH)* increases the probability of opting for one of the two types of private schools. This suggests that, all else being constant, the higher the level of education of the head of the household, the greater the probability that the family will opt for private education for their children. This result is consistent with the high level of concern

---

[7] Head of household occupation classification is based on worker's status as white collar or blue collar worker.

Table 2.13. Econometric Results of the Model

Variable	Subsidized Private Schools[1]	Tuition-supported Private Schools[1]
CONSTANT	-1.79	-5.98
	(0.24)	(0.75)
CNTMN17	-0.15	-0.13
	(0.25E-1)	(0.64E-1)
TOTALH	0.14E-5	0.34E-5
	(0.43E-6)	(0.65E-6)
ESCJEFH	0.35E-1	0.26
	(0.99E-2)	(0.26E-1)
EXIAEDUC	0.61E-1	0.19
	(0.12E-1)	(0.30E-1)
DEXISPJA	-0.26	-2.21
	(0.13)	(0.39)
DZ	1.59	1.09
	(0.21)	(0.66)
DESTADO	-0.49E-3	-0.82E-3
	(0.33E-3)	(0.46E-3)
Log Likelihood	-3584.3	-3584.3
Restricted Log Likelihood[2]	-4360.4	-4360.4
No. Observations	4667.0	4667.0

Source: Authors' calculations.
Notes: [1] The standard deviations are in parentheses.
        [2] Refers to the model with gradient equal to zero.

parents with higher levels of education have for providing their children with a good education. A similar result is obtained in the case of the variable that measures the level of education of the mother *(EXIAEDUC)*.

All else being constant, two-parent households *(DEXISPJA)* have a lower probability of choosing a private education for the children, either in a subsidized or a tuition-supported private school. On the other hand, children in urban households *(DZ)* have a higher probability of attending private school than children in rural households. This can be attributed to the lower number of private schools in rural areas.

Table 2.14. Estimated Basic Regression Parameters
(Dependent Variable: Log of SIMCE Scores for 4th grade Spanish)

Independent variables	OLS[1] Parameter (t-statistic)	Truncated OLS[2] Parameter (t-statistic)
Constant	3.270048	3.2701
	(29.238)	(29.364)
Ratio	0.003323	0.003323
	(5.076)	(5.098)
Pdoc	0.001696	0.001696
	(3.111)	(3.126)
Padm	0.004134	0.004131
	(1.204)	(1.208)
Aeducy	0.012875	0.012872
	(3.803)	(3.818)
Indpob	-0.00583	-0.00583
	(-4.342)	(-4.362)
Deps	0.085383	0.08538
	(8.795)	(8.833)
Depp	0.252819	0.25283
	(15.590)	(15.659)
Taprob4	0.61178	0.6118
	(5.790)	(5.816)
Trprob4	-0.20536	-0.20535
	(-1.474)	(-1.480)
Standard deviation		0.133
		(47.916)
R^2	0.5232	
Adjusted R^2	0.5194	
F-statistic	138.74	
Likelihood log		687.07

Source: Authors' calculations.
Notes: [1] Ordinary least squares approximation.
[2] Ordinary least squares approximation for the truncated sample. Truncation occurs when the SIMCE score reaches the value of 100 since this is the maximum attainable score.

In the case of an unhealthy child *(DESTADO)*, all else being equal, the probability of attending a private school is reduced. This result is consistent with the lower academic performance that might be expected from children with health problems. Parents of these children would probably expect a diminished return on their investment, and therefore, would be less willing to pay for a superior education.

Policy Lessons from the Chilean Experience

The following section groups the main policy lessons derived from Chile's experience with social service delivery. The topics reviewed are coverage and qual-

**Table 2.15. Estimated Basic Regression Parameters
(Dependent Variable: Log of SIMCE Scores for 4th Grade Mathematics)**

Independent Variables	OLS[1] Parameter (t-statistic)	Truncated OLS[2] Parameter (t-statistic)
Constant	3.294182	3.2942
	(28.506)	(28.629)
Ratio	0.003023	0.003022
	(4.469)	(4.488)
Pdoc	0.002028	0.002029
	(3.601)	(3.617)
Padm	0.005787	0.005783
	(1.631)	(1.637)
Aeducy	0.016802	0.016799
	(4.804)	(4.822)
Pvind	-0.00471	-0.00471
	(-3.400)	(-3.416)
Deps	0.094574	0.09457
	(9.429)	(9.469)
Detp	0.269575	0.26959
	(16.088)	(16.160)
Taprob4	0.510114	0.51014
	(4.673)	(4.693)
Trprob4	-0.28515	-0.28513
	(-1.981)	(-1.989)
Standard Deviation		0.13742
		(47.916)
R2	0.5273	
Adjusted R2	0.5235	
F-statistic	141.03	
Likelihood log		649.52

Source: Authors' calculations.
Notes: [1] Ordinary least squares approximation.
    [2] Ordinary least squares approximation for the truncated sample. Truncation occurs when
    the SIMCE score reaches the value of 100 since this is the maximum attainable score.

ity, targeting, cost recovery, decentralization, fiscal transfer mechanisms, private delivery, networks, and information on social policy design.

Coverage and Quality

Social service delivery is adequate. Universal coverage is provided in preschool, elementary, and high school education; in-patient and out-patient care; and the PNAC. The coverage encompasses almost everyone who desires the derived benefits.

**Table 2.16. Estimated Basic Regression Parameters
(Dependent Variable: Log of SIMCE Scores for 8th Grade Spanish)**

Independent Variables	OLS[1] Parameter (t-statistic)	Truncated OLS[2] Parameter (t-statistic)
Constant	3.41382	3.4138
	(55.702)	(55.891)
Ratio	0.004651	0.004651
	(6.693)	(6.717)
Pdoc	0.003179	0.003179
	(5.923)	(5.945)
Aeducy	0.013962	0.013962
	(3.908)	(3.921)
Indpob	-0.00540	-0.00540
	(-3.796)	(-3.810)
Deps	0.090241	0.090235
	(9.023)	(9.054)
Depp	0.331205	0.33122
	(19.980)	(20.051)
Taprob8	0.206141	0.20616
	(4.236)	(4.251)
Standard Deviation		0.14078
		(47.707)
R^2	0.4962	
Adjusted R^2	0.4931	
F-statistic	158.99	
Likelihood log		616.36

Source: Authors' calculations.
Notes: [1] Ordinary least squares approximation.
   [2] Ordinary least squares approximation for the truncated sample. Truncation occurs when the SIMCE score reaches the value of 100 since this is the maximum attainable score.

Financial subsidy programs and the PAE are targeted: they benefit only a portion of the population. In this regard, budgetary constraints have limited financial subsidy coverage (SUF and PASIS) to around 50 percent of potential beneficiaries.

In addition, the consensus is that the quality of the services supplied in the area of health and education is inadequate. Several different factors contribute to this: obsolete technologies, depreciated infrastructure, poorly paid and unmotivated personnel, and overall shortcomings in the design of the social programs.

The subject of quality is complex and requires a comprehensive approach. For example, raising salaries of those who work in the different programs will have a positive effect only if accompanied by measures that link performance to income and make hiring and firing conditions more flexible.

**Table 2.17. Estimated Basic Regression Parameters
(Dependent Variable: Log of SIMCE for 8th Grade Mathematics)**

Independent Variables	OLS[1] Parameter (t-statistic)	Truncated OLS[2] Parameter (t-statistic)
Constant	3.372412 (54.161)	3.3724 (54.351)
Ratio	0.004018 (4.526)	0.004018 (4.542)
Pdoc	0.002985 (4.354)	0.002985 (4.370)
Indpob	-0.00823 (-5.578)	-0.00823 (-5.597)
Totinc	0.000139 (2.833)	0.000139 (2.843)
Deps	0.081946 (6.434)	0.08194 (6.457)
Depp	0.401922 (18.184)	0.40192 (18.248)
Taprob8	0.296696 (4.780)	0.2967 (4.797)
Standard Deviation		0.17956 (47.707)
R2	0.4534	
Adjusted R2	0.45	
F-statistic	133.38	
Likelihood log		339.47

Source: Authors' calculations.
Notes: [1] Ordinary least squares approximation.
[2] Ordinary least squares approximation for the truncated sample. Truncation occurs when the SIMCE score reaches the value of 100 since this is the maximum attainable score.

Targeting

Financial subsidy programs, which account for 18 percent of social spending, are generally carefully targeted through mechanisms that identify socioeconomic and personal characteristics (age, pregnancy, physical or mental handicaps). Nutritional programs are targeted on the basis of personal characteristics. In the case of PNAC, targeting takes place through a process of self-selection, while the PAE uses criteria based on socioeconomic indicators.

The use of targeting mechanisms has generally been adequate and has resulted in programs that have been quite efficient. An exception is family allowance, a kind of blanket subsidy that has been costly and inefficient since it provided fiscal assistance to high-income sectors not needing the help. In recent years, this subsidy has been recalibrated to correct the situation.

Targeting of universal programs, such as health and elementary education, has occurred through a process of self-selection, whereby high-income individuals have preferred subscribing to better and costlier private services.

Cost Recovery

Universal coverage of health and education programs should not be confused with free access to these services. Cases may vary according to individual programs. Health programs are mainly financed through beneficiary contributions, consisting of monthly premium fees and a co-payment fee at the time the service is received. This structure combines efficiency in treating risks with equity since fees are based on subscriber income levels. Public pre-school, elementary, and secondary education, however, is free. This approach appears to be inefficient in the context of an education system characterized by inferior quality and lack of resources, and by higher-income families willing to pay for a better education. On the other hand, higher education is funded by fiscal contributions that are allocated, in part, to subsidize teaching personnel, while universities are funded largely through tuition fees.

Decentralization

One of the most important reforms was the decentralization of social programs in education and health. However, decentralization has been more of a formality than a reality. For example, during a 10-year period, only 18 percent of schools have chosen to adapt their curricula to reflect characteristics of their student populations, their geographical locations, and other traits. The remaining 82 percent of the schools have chosen to adopt a centralized model promoted by the ministry. In practice, health care services continue to be centralized, even in those areas in which they are legally autonomous.

There are several reasons for the lack of autonomy in the health and education sectors. Chief among them are the lack of personnel training and motivation, shortcomings that are linked to the shortage of clear incentives that reward superior management in education and health care. Moreover, decentralization was carried out for the first 10 years under an authoritarian regime that centralized policy decisions. Obviously, this limited the actual degree of autonomy and community participation in social programs.

Decentralization in the health sector has been particularly slow because of financial constraints. The civil servant status of hospital workers makes salary schedules and facility levels dependent on external factors. Also, budget allocations for supplies are subject to preestablished macroeconomic assumptions and negotiations between the central and regional authorities.

Fiscal Transfer Mechanisms

Resource allocation mechanisms in the social sectors have produced mixed results. The subsidy system in education seems to be a simple, efficient, and cost-effective way to transfer fiscal resources to pre-school, elementary, and secondary education.

However, the subsidy system has been limited in its most interesting application to subsidize demand for competition among providers of educational services. Parents have not had access to results of scholastic achievement tests, and were thus denied vital information for making educational decisions. This has been the result of pressures from teacher organizations, which are concerned about job security; apprehensions of the sector's intellectuals and sector officials about parents' freedom to choose a school; and concerns about the equity of such subsidies.

This study presents indirect evidence that supports the effectiveness of a demand subsidy system. In fact, it has been shown that, all else being equal, subsidized private schools produce better results than their municipal counterparts. Even though they receive equal assistance, subsidized private schools must be able to attract students if they want to stay in operation. Municipal schools, on the other hand, have a mandate to provide education and are able to rely on special allocations when enrollments fall short. Thus, the subsidy mechanism operates with greater transparency in the private subsidized system than in the municipal system. The better results shown for the former schools validate, therefore, the effectiveness of their subsidy system.

The allocation of fiscal resources to higher education is diversified. However, the effectiveness of the sector's institutions is impaired because of preference given to direct contributions not based on performance.

Fiscal allocation mechanisms for the health sector, FAP and FAPEM, have been adversely affected by their dependence on predetermined budgets and on an outdated and overvalued cost structure for services. These mechanisms are very complex because of the diversity in services provided and the nature of the health market itself. In any event, the health sector has operated under a supply-subsidy system. Hospitals and primary care centers receive resources regardless of the quality of their services. This accounts for the public's negative view of the health system concerning available resources and poor quality in care and treatment. For this reason the set of reforms under study include mechanisms that bring beneficiaries into the process that decides resource allocations within the sector.

Private Delivery

Two interesting lessons can be learned from the experiences related to private delivery of social services. First, it has been generally shown that, after adjusting for the effects of other variables, educational services provided by publicly subsidized private schools are better than those of municipal institutions. Hence, private delivery has made a positive contribution to publicly funded education.

Second, in health, the emergence of private insurance companies (ISAPRE) has brought about important changes in public health care. It has been shown that a redistributive public system is inconsistent with a private system that provides benefits based on subscriber contributions. Indeed, ISAPRE was partly responsible for the massive exodus from the public system of high-income subscribers who were cross-subsidizing the poorer beneficiaries in the system. Employment alternatives in the private sector also raised expectations for higher salaries for the medical and paramedical work force. Consequently, Chile's public health service is faced with the dual challenge of increasing worker incomes while coping with diminishing revenues.

Networks

The experience of linking social programs has been successful. Food programs were integrated into networks that supplemented them with health control and school assistance. This has enhanced nutrition, hygiene, and educational objectives. Moreover, enrollment in certain social programs was useful in the targeting of others.

Information systems

The implementation of measurement, evaluation, and control systems has been essential for improving the efficiency of Chile's social policy. The CASEN survey that measures the distribution of social programs and the socioeconomic accreditation mechanisms tied to financial subsidies and food programs (CAS record and PAE socioeconomic index) are important examples. Also crucial were the development of appropriate diagnoses of the need for social programs. For example, policies effectively designed on the basis of the nutrition and health profiles of the population were responsible for the excellent results in nutrition and maternal-infant health care. The changing nature of the profiles makes it necessary, however, to monitor constantly and introduce necessary changes in the social policies.

BIBLIOGRAPHY

Casassus, J. 1989. Decentralization and Deconcentration of Educational Systems in Latin America: Foundations and Critical Aspects. Paper presented at conference, the Interagency Meeting, Decentralization and Deconcentration of Public Policy, Brazil.

Castañeda, T. 1991. *Para combatir la pobreza.* Santiago: Centro de Estudios Públicos.

Edwards, V., J. Assaél, and G. López. 1991. *Directores y maestros en la escuela municipalizada.* Santiago: Programa Interdisciplinario de Investigaciones en Educacíón (PIIE).

Espínola, V. 1991. *Decentralización del sistema escolar en Chile.* Santiago: Centro de Investigación y Desarrollo de la Educación (CIDE).

Haindl, E., E. Budinich, and I. Irarrázaval. 1989. *Gasto social efectivo.* Santiago: Oficina de Planificación (ODEPLAN) and the University of Chile.

Henríquez, G.P. 1991. El sistema de subvenciones vigente en Chile. Ministerio de Educación (MINEDUC). Santiago, Chile. Mimeo.

Latorre, C.L., I. Núñez, L.E. Gonzáles, *et al.* 1991. *La municipalización de la educación: una mirada desde los administradores del sistema.* Santiago: PIIE.

Levin, H.M. 1991. The Economics of Educational Chile. *Economics of Education Review* 10 (2): 137-158.

Magendzo, A., L. Egaña, and C.L. Latorre. 1988. *La educación particular y los esquemas privatizantes en educación bajo un estado subsidiario, 1973-1987.* Santiago: PIIE.

Ministerio de Planificación (MIDEPLAN). 1991a. *Propuesta de acción en alimentación y nutrición.* Santiago: MIDEPLAN.

———. 1991b. *Un proceso de integración al desarrollo. Informe social 90/91.* Santiago: MIDEPLAN.

———. 1991c. Evolución y distribución del gasto social en Chile. Santiago, Chile. Mimeo.

————. 1991d. Problématica y proposiciones sobre subsidios monetarios SUF y PASIS. Santiago, Chile. Mimeo.

————. 1992a. *Población, educación, vivienda, salud, empleo y pobreza, CASEN 1990*. Santiago: MIDEPLAN.

————. 1992b. *Impacto distributivo de los subsidios monetarios, CASEN 1990*. Santiago: MIDEPLAN.

————. 1992c. *Avanzando en equidad. Un proceso de integración al desarrollo: 1990-1992*. Santiago: MIDEPLAN.

————. 1992d. *Los sistemas previsionales de salud*. Santiago: MIDEPLAN.

————. 1993. Programas sociales: su impacto en los hogares chilenos. (In print). Santiago: MIDEPLAN.

Ministerio de Educación (MINEDUC). 1991. *Compendio información estadística, 1990*. Santiago: MINEDUC.

Ministerio de Salud (MINSAL). 1992a. *Estudio de asignación de recursos financieros al interior del sistema público de salud*. Santiago: MINSAL.

————. 1992b. *Recuperación de costos*. Santiago: MINSAL.

————. 1992c. *Apoyo al desarrollo institucional del Ministerio de Salud y Servicios de Salud*. Santiago: MINSAL.

Miranda, E. 1990. *Decentralización y privatización del sistema de salud*. Estudios Públicos No. 39. Santiago, Chile.

Mujica, P., and O. Larrañaga. 1992. *Distribución de ingresos y políticas sociales en Chile*. Santiago: ILADES-Georgetown.

Raczynski, D. 1991. La ficha CAS y la focalización de los programas sociales. Santiago, Chile. Mimeo.

Torche, A. 1990. Algunas reflexiones sobre la situación nutricional en Chile. *Cuadernos de economía* (No. 81). Santiago, Chile.

————. 1985. Una evaluación del Programa Nacional de Alimentación Complementaria (PNAC). *Cuadernos de Economía* (No. 66). Santiago, Chile.

Vial, I., and R. Camhi. 1991. Experiencias y dilemas en la focalización del Programa Nacional de Alimentación Complementaria, Instituto Libertad y Desarrollo, Santiago. Mimeo.

The World Bank. 1991. *Staff Appraisal Report, Chile, Primary Education Improvement Project.* Washington, D.C.: The World Bank.

―――. 1989. *Social Development Progress in Chile: Achievements and Challenges.* Washington, D.C.: The World Bank.

CHAPTER THREE

ENHANCING SOCIAL SERVICES
IN COSTA RICA

Juan Diego Trejos, Leonardo Garnier,
Guillermo Monge, and Roberto Hidalgo

Costa Rica has enjoyed a long tradition of state-funded direct social services rooted in a broad national consensus on the relevance and soundness of this policy. The state's participation in service delivery began when it attempted to make elementary education and, later, health services universally available through state programs designed to expand opportunities and encourage competition. The programs were supplemented by initiatives aimed at offsetting existing inequities and, thereby, improving the effectiveness, efficiency, and equity of social policy.

As the indicators presented in Table 3.1 show, Costa Rica's investment in its population's quality of life has been highly successful and has placed the country in a privileged position. Despite these obvious successes, however, the country's social service system has had, and continues to have, several problems. These problems worsened during the eighties as a result of budgetary constraints, the emergence of new challenges in global economic integration, and the erosion of public programs and institutions.

The purpose of this chapter is two-fold: first, to highlight the factors that contributed to the success of the country's social services delivery system; and, second, to identify the system's major problems and challenges and propose reforms that would enhance its efficiency and equity. This balanced approach, rather than a one-sided analysis of the achievements or shortcomings of a particular social service program, will allow pragmatic lessons to be drawn. These lessons, when taken in the historical context of individual countries, could prove useful in the reform of other social policies in the region.

The main lesson derived from the Costa Rican experience is that there are no easy, unilateral solutions when it comes to social policy. It is clear that state involvement does not always guarantee an efficient solution when dealing with social problems—particularly those affecting society's poorest segment—and that poor management of social programs can upset delicate financial equilibria.

Table 3.1. Indicators of Positive Impact in the Social Sectors

	Countries with a high level of human development[1]			
Indicator	Developed Countries	Developing Countries	Latin America	Costa Rica
Number of countries	33	16	9	—
Health				
Life expectancy[2]	74.5	70.5	70.3	74.9
Infant mortality[2]	13.0	33.0	34.9	18.0
Deaths < 5 years of age	18.0	40.0	42.3	22.0
Education				
Adult literacy[3]	99.0	91.0	89.9	92.8
Years of school	10.0	6.6	6.0	5.7
Social Welfare				
Low birth weight	n/a	10.0	8.5	6.0
Indigent population	n/a	n/a	26.5	23.6
Real GDP (PPA US$)[2]	15,043	6,027	5,379	4,413

Source: United Nations Development Programme, UNDP (1992) and ECLAC (1992).
Notes: 1 With human development index equal to or greater than 0.8.
2 Per 1,000
3 Percentage of population
4 Gross domestic product expressed in purchasing power parity (UNDP, 1992)

However, it is also clear that in the case of Costa Rica, government policies have been largely responsible for the social progress achieved by the country during the past four decades. Thus, this study does not advocate dismantling Costa Rica's social service policy, which could serve as a model for others and which has largely been the cornerstone of the country's political system, but, rather, advocates its reform. This reform, as shall be seen, emphasizes issues related to the financing, efficiency, and distribution of social programs. At the same time, the reform conforms with Costa Rica's tradition of consensus in shaping programs. It views social services as a public-interest good and related financial outlays as high-return investments. The study focuses on services in health, education, and welfare, emphasizing in the latter services that mobilize resources and provide extensive coverage. In 1991, the total budget for the three sectors was approximately $730 million, which represented 65 percent of public social spending, 78 percent of social spending (excluding pension payments), 33 percent of combined nonfinancial public sector spending, and 13 percent of gross domestic product (GDP).[1]

---

1 Amounts are in U.S. dollars unless otherwise noted.

Table 3.2. Relative Size of Programs Studied Based on Public Spending, 1991
(percent)

Programs and subprograms	Percent of total	Percent of sector
Education services	35.9	100.0
Lower education	21.2	58.5
Pre-school	1.3	3.5
Elementary	12.5	34.5
Secondary	7.4	20.5
Professional training	2.7	7.6
Higher education	12.3	33.9
Junior college	0.3	0.9
University	12.0	33.0
Health services	54.4	100.0
Primary care	5.2	9.5
Curative care	44.9	82.6
Outpatient consultation	20.4	37.5
Hospitalization	24.5	45.1
Water and sanitation	4.3	7.8
Social Welfare Services	9.7	100.0
Food assistance	4.3	44.4
Pre-school	2.8	28.4
School	1.3	13.5
Indigent	0.2	2.5
Cash transfers	5.4	55.6
Pensions	1.6	16.7
Housing subsidy	3.8	38.9

Source: Ministry of Finance, Technical Secretariat of the Budget Office.

In terms of budgetary outlays, it can be seen from Table 3.2 that health services represented the largest percentage of expenditures in 1991. The sector accounted for 54 percent of total spending, 83 percent of which was for medical treatment. Following in importance were education services, which represented 36 percent of social spending and which, when combined with health spending, accounted for 90 percent of the entire social sector budget. Elementary and university education each accounted for one-third of the sector's resources, while secondary education accounted for one-fifth. Spending associated with professional training rose slightly, capturing 8 percent of the sector's resources. This service, however, is not included in this study.

Allocations for social welfare programs accounted for the remaining 10 percent of social spending. Resources for this sector were spread evenly between two large categories: food assistance and cash transfers.

Health Services

Institutional Structure of Health Services

Pressures dating back to the early 1900s to establish workers' medical care programs and social insurance schemes intensified during the difficult 1930s and culminated in 1941 with the social reforms that led to the creation of the Costa Rican Social Security Fund (CCSS). Since that time, progress has been almost uninterrupted. However, the most significant advances occurred in the 1960s when the first National Health Plans were drafted, universal coverage instituted, and the health sector formally created under the oversight of a ministry. The National Health Plans adopted at that time attempted to define health as a public good under state regulation and to create a single, comprehensive system; to achieve universal coverage through rural, community, and environmental health and nutrition programs; and to implement countrywide health care coverage through the CCSS (MIDEPLAN, 1992).

As the sector's overseer, the Ministry of Health is responsible for formulating national health policies and related regulations and for coordinating all public and private health care activities. The ministry is also responsible for the development and promotion of health, as well as for disease prevention and environmental control. The CCSS is the agency responsible for managing compulsory and state social insurance programs. It is also responsible for providing medical treatment and recovery and rehabilitation services, and for cooperating with the ministry in the promotion of health and prevention of disease.

Coverage and Impact of Health Services

Health Spending

Health care in Costa Rica relies on three sources of financing. Health and maternity insurance is financed through worker-employer assessments, to which the state contributes. The current premiums on assessable wages are 5.5 percent for workers and 9.25 percent for employers. The state's contribution is 0.25 percent.

The state also finances preventive care and medical treatment provided by the Ministry of Health. In this type of financing, a large proportion of available resources depends on the level of economic activity and not only on the policies of ruling governments or on the situation of public finances.

Indeed, the systematic growth in public health and nutrition spending between 1940 and 1980 was similar to that for the economy as a whole. By the mid-1970s, public outlays for health and nutrition accounted for 20 percent of total spending and 7.5 percent of GDP. Emphasis on health policies during the 1970s greatly stimulated spending on health and nutrition, causing it to grow at an average annual rate of 15 percent in real terms between 1976 and 1979, when it accounted for 25 percent of total spending and 10.5 percent of GDP. Obviously, this also meant a significant increase in per capita health and nutrition spending, which grew by 37 percent between 1977 and 1979.

By then, however, the adverse impacts of the economic crisis had begun to be felt. Real spending in health and nutrition fell by 36 percent between 1979 and 1982, with its contribution to total public spending decreasing by 11 percent and accounting for only 5 percent of GDP. Per capita spending in health and nutrition declined steadily from 1979 to 1985, when it amounted to only 51 percent of the 1979 peak level. The plunge in social spending—particularly for health and nutrition—leveled off in 1982, and spending began to climb in 1985. However, spending levels at the end of the decade were still well below those achieved at the end of the 1970s. Table 3.3 shows that in 1991 Costa Rica allocated the equivalent of 14 percent of total spending and 6.2 percent of GDP to the health sector (Garnier, 1991; Coto, 1992).

Health Service Coverage

Despite the effect of the crisis and budgetary constraints during the 1980s, program coverage remained relatively unchanged. Coverage in the early 1990s was similar to that in the late 1970s. Health and maternity coverage, which rose from 58 percent in 1970 to 92 percent in 1980, fluctuated around the latter level throughout the decade. In 1991, coverage was available for 2,748,901 Costa Ricans, representing 89 percent of the country's population (CCSS, Technical Office for Actuarial and Institutional Planning).

The Ministry of Health's rural health program was seriously impaired by the crisis. Coverage for the program, which rose from 11 percent of rural population in 1973 (year program started) to 61 percent in 1979, dropped to 52 percent in 1981. Coverage levels began recovering that year, and by 1988 reached 65 percent of rural population. Coverage for community health programs rose from 10 percent of urban population in 1976 (year program started) to 63 percent in 1979 but fell to 40 percent in 1984. A slow recovery began that year, and by 1987, coverage rose to 47 percent of urban population (Miranda, 1988).

Table 3.3. Evolution of Public Health Spending, 1983-91
(millions of current colones)

	Current	Real[1]	% of total	% of GDP	Per capita real[1]
1983	7,032	100.0	11.4	5.4	100.0
1984	8,136	103.4	11.0	5.0	93.7
1985	9,722	108.0	15.5	4.9	94.4
1986	13,094	129.4	11.3	5.3	112.7
1987	15,834	133.9	12.8	5.6	115.2
1988	20,568	143.9	13.7	5.9	119.7
1989	25,846	155.2	13.7	6.1	128.6
1990	32,868	165.8	14.2	6.3	134.0
1991	42,190	165.4	14.0	6.2	129.1

Source: Technical Secretariat of the Second Bipartisan Commission for the Reform of the Costa Rican State (COREC) II.
Note: [1] Growth index based on 1983.

Information on privately sponsored medical services is scarce. The Social Security Fund is responsible for most hospital services, contributing 96 percent of all hospital payments. According to a recent study (Kleysen, 1988), private sector health spending in 1986 represented 25 percent of public sector spending, with the Red Cross and a telethon being major private contributors to spending. Similar conclusions can be drawn from the 1988 National Income and Spending Survey, which shows that the private sector accounted for 23 percent of total health spending (Sáenz and León, 1992).

Health Spending Allocations

In terms of social distribution, the wealthiest quintile of the population accounted for more than half of private health spending (53 percent), while the poorest quintile accounted for less than 4 percent. Overall, the poorest 60 percent of the population accounted for one-quarter of private health spending, while the wealthiest 40 percent contributed the remaining three-quarters. Diagnostic and hospitalization services show an even larger disparity. For these services, the poorest 20 percent of the population accounted for less than 2 percent of private spending, while the wealthiest 20 percent accounted for more than 80 percent (Sáenz and León, 1992).

This pattern of private spending on health contrasts significantly with the progressive nature of public spending. In terms of regional distribution, the most recent studies indicate that 46 percent of state health program subsidies went to urban areas, and 54 percent to rural areas. This is particularly significant if we take into account that at that time 52 percent of the population lived in urban

Table 3.4. Distribution of Families Benefiting from Public Health Spending, 1986

Quintile[1]	Total	Food and nutrition	Hospita- lization	Outpatient consultation	Preventive medicine
I	27.7	39.0	27.8	22.3	27.8
II	23.5	27.2	23.1	22.4	24.1
III	24.1	18.1	26.2	24.5	19.1
IV	13.8	11.0	12.0	18.1	16.6
V	10.8	4.7	10.9	12.7	12.4
Total	100.0	100.0	100.0	100.0	100.0

Source: World Bank (1990b).
Note: Quintile I represents the lowest level of income; quintile V, the highest.

zones and 48 percent in rural areas. An even stronger bias in favor of rural areas is seen in preventive health care, with more than 60 percent of this sector's spending being targeted to rural areas. These areas also consumed 53 percent of spending on medical treatment (Rodríguez, 1986).

As to distribution by income levels, all available information shows that public spending on health and nutrition is clearly progressive. Three-quarters of the families who benefitted from these services belonged to the poorest 60 percent of the population, while only one-fourth of the beneficiaries belonged to the wealthiest two quintiles. Of the families who received health care services, 28 percent were in the poorest quintile, while only 11 percent were in the wealthiest quintile (see Table 3.4). The poorest 20 percent of the country's families received 22.3 percent of outpatient care, 27.8 percent of preventive and hospital care, and 39 percent of food and nutrition services.

The distribution of this spending is even more apparent when one considers that incomes for the poorest 10 percent of the population increased by 61 percent as a result of subsidies received from health services. The contribution to income was even greater in rural areas, where the subsidies represented 78 percent of incomes of the poorest 10 percent. On the other hand, the wealthiest 10 percent of the population received a subsidy equivalent to only 2 percent of their income. This smaller percent can be explained by both the higher incomes and smaller subsidies of this group. The poorest 10 percent received 17 percent of the total health spending subsidies, while the wealthiest 10 percent received only 9 percent. These differences are also evident when the data are grouped differently. Only 13 percent of health care subsidies were received by the wealthiest quintiles, whose incomes increased 2.4 percent, while 30 percent of the subsidies were received by the poorest quintile, whose incomes grew, as a result, by 41 percent. The poorest 60 percent of the population received 70 percent of the subsidy, while the wealthiest 40 percent received only 30 percent (Rodríguez, 1986).

The Impact of Health Services

Universal insurance coverage and the development of rural and community health programs in the 1970s helped reduce general mortality from 6.6 to 4.1 per thousand, infant mortality from 61.5 to 19 per thousand, and neonatal mortality from 24.8 to 11.2 per thousand. Significant changes were also recorded in death and disease patterns. For example, mortality from diarrheal ailments dropped from 70 per 100 thousand inhabitants to only 5.2, and in 1980 these diseases ranked as the 15th cause of death, down from the first.[2] Despite the economic difficulties experienced by Costa Rica during the 1980s and the problems that affected the health sector as a result, the general mortality rate continued to improve slowly, settling at 3.8 deaths per thousand by the end of 1990.

As Table 3.5 shows, the incidence of most causes of death remained relatively stable throughout the 1980s, thereby consolidating the changes in the country's epidemiological profile that began in the 1970s. The impact of the economic crisis, however, was substantial. During the 1980s, several diseases that had been virtually eradicated in Costa Rica (such as malaria, measles, mumps, and German measles) reappeared, and the incidence of infant malnutrition also increased.

In summary, Costa Rica's health system today faces challenges that are largely attributable to its own success. Indeed, changes in the size and make-up of its population, as well as 40 years of changes in the country's epidemiological profile, present a picture of needs that are totally different from those for which the current system was designed.

Problems and Challenges of the Health Sector

Epidemiological changes, the impact of the economic crisis, and the resulting stabilization process created financial constraints and altered Costa Rica's demand for health services. As a result, Costa Rica's health care system had to take emergency measures to avoid financial bankruptcy and restricted coverage. While these measures allowed these basic objectives to be met successfully, they did so at the high cost of deteriorated services and loss of the strategic direction established in the 1970s.

Quality of Service and Care Model

The attempt to maintain health service coverage without making institutional changes that would address the above problems caused the costs of these prob-

---

2 Unless otherwise indicated, the data for this section was provided by the Ministry of Health, Department of Statistics.

Table 3.5. Mortality by Cause, Selected Years
(levels and rate per 10,000 inhabitants)

	1970	Rate	1980	Rate	1990	Rate
Infectious and parasitic	2,362	13.6	348	1.5	392	1.3
Tumors	1,146	6.6	1,549	6.8	2,255	7.5
Glandular and immunological	281	1.6	307	1.3	359	1.2
Blood-related	121	0.7	39	0.2	59	0.2
Mental	62	0.4	53	0.2	45	0.1
Nervous	173	1.0	156	0.7	247	0.8
Circulatory	2,243	13.0	2,347	10.3	3,157	10.5
Respiratory	1,548	9.2	944	4.1	1,210	4.0
Digestive	429	2.5	426	1.9	533	1.8
Genitourinary	124	0.7	156	0.7	308	1.0
Pregnancy	55	1.0	16	0.2	12	0.1
Skin	27	0.2	28	0.1	90	0.3
Osteomuscular	27	0.2	24	0.1	44	0.1
Congenital	183	1.1	309	1.4	375	1.2
Perinatal	643	3.7	550	2.4	531	1.8
Deformity	1,281	7.4	784	3.4	428	1.4
External	763	4.4	1,237	5.4	1,321	4.4
TOTAL	11,504	66.5	9,273	40.7	11,366	37.7

Source: Ministry of Health, Department and Statistics.

lems to be transferred in unforeseen ways to beneficiaries. Among these are long waiting lists that increasingly limit access to out-patient services, alarmingly long waiting periods for specialized medical services, shorter patient consultations, slow laboratory and diagnostic services, and a lack of CCSS pharmacological supplies.

This deterioration is fostering unofficial privatized health services. In some cases, waiting lists and poor care force patients to seek private consultations with public health doctors. Even more serious are the private fees doctors charge depending on the type of preferential treatment they provide. One of the most widespread forms of corruption is the "biombo" system in which Health Fund doctors provide services to their private patients using public facilities and resources. Under this system, in which the doctor uses the institution for private (and lucrative) gain, patients avoid the red tape and waiting lists that the insured must endure and are subsidized at the expense of the Social Security Fund.

The only way to avoid these problems without having to abandon national health system objectives is to recognize the limitations of a health care program that, in response to the financial crisis and changes in the country's epidemiological profile, has overemphasized medical treatment. At the same time, it is important to regain the direction set in the 1970s that reflected an integrated view of health care. As one recent document affirms, it is necessary to "adopt a family and community health model characterized by comprehensive and continuous care for the individual, the family, the community, and the environment; by community participation in diagnosing, programming, controlling and evaluating health services; by interdisciplinary teamwork and by mechanisms that guarantee quality and allow an evaluation of the consequences of health-related actions (Weinstock, *et al.*, 1992)." It is in this context that the following proposals must be fully understood.

Political Supervision and Institutional Coordination

Attempts to establish an integrated National Health System that would operate under the supervision of the Ministry of Health were unsuccessful. The institutional scheme now in place does not allow the ministry to exercise authority effectively, to define the sector's political priorities, or to establish different tiers of responsibility in implementing health policies.

Despite the efforts made during the last decades to integrate the system, particularly health services provided by the CCSS and the ministry, the process is still in its formative stages. Enforcing integration within an environment characterized by loss of strategic direction and severe financial constraints has paradoxically resulted in an emphasis on medical treatment, which because of its greater urgency over preventive care had already prevailed in the system (Sanguinetti, 1988).

The Ministry of Health needs to discharge its duties efficiently as overseer of the sector. The ministry must become an effective supervisory entity, equipped with the necessary technical, financial, and political capacity for defining priorities, formulating policies, establishing directives, providing political coordination for institutions within its sector, and evaluating and controlling program results. In addition, the ministry must continue to foster integration of services and elimination of redundancies. For the process to succeed, however, it must be carried out with a great deal of pragmatism, whereby consideration is given to specific requirements of individual situations.

Administrative and Management Practices

Management practices in the health sector are obsolete. In general, the system is characterized by practices that are task-oriented rather than goal-oriented. Management practices and high-level positions have become tools for exerting labor and personal power within institutions. Struggles for institutional power between doctors and administrators have tended to reinforce the medical treatment bias of health policies, thus contributing to the overall inflexibility and inefficiency of the system.

Excessive hierarchies are another obsolete feature of the Costa Rican health system. Despite efforts to decentralize and make the system more flexible, there is still little decision-making latitude at the regional and local levels of health care.

On a technical level, efforts should first be aimed at increasing managerial and administrative professionalism and, second, at encouraging adequate distribution and decentralization of health services. These efforts should be carried out based on the principles of the proposed integrated health care model.

Given the great deal of experience acquired by the rural and community health sectors and the fact that a large part of the country's health infrastructure is concentrated there, one of the first steps that should be taken is the reconstitution, expansion, and strengthening of rural and community health programs. Distribution and decentralization of health services could also be achieved by establishing an efficient network of local health systems (SILOS). This would entail creating health districts as basic administrative units for the SILOS, gradually strengthening and unifying regional and local health authorities and granting local authorities greater management and budgetary autonomy. In this regard, a most interesting suggestion is to create in each health area basic comprehensive health care teams (*equipos básicos de atención integral,* EBAIs). These teams, made up of a doctor, a nurse, and a health care assistant, would be responsible for providing care in regional sectors containing three or four thousand inhabitants within their area. The teams would rely on the equipment and assistance of the most highly qualified personnel of the country's more sophisticated clinics and hospital centers and on a network of assistance services tailored to field requirements. The teams could also rely on private health facilities, thereby increasing the flexibility of the system and reducing its fixed costs (Weinstock *et al.,* 1992).

Incentives and Human Resource Policy

While Costa Rica has a large number of qualified health care professionals, the lack of a well-defined human resource policy has created significant imbalances within the sector. Emphasis on medical specialization, at the expense of general practice and basic health care training, has greatly impaired the allocation of medical resources to different levels of the health sector. As a result, there is a notable shortage of nursing personnel, and doctors outnumber nurses in the country's hospitals and clinics. Other problems facing the health system stem from the ineffective use of human resources, absenteeism, favoritism, and system abuse by individuals seeking personal gain.

Many of these shortcomings reflect a lack of adequate incentives within the system and management practices that fail to evaluate results. The latter has given rise to shabby practices in personnel management that, in turn, have been aggravated by misplaced labor interests. A first step in confronting these problems would be to decentralize management and establish a modern, professional system that would provide appropriate training and human resource allocation for meeting the needs and objectives of the proposed comprehensive health care model. Within this new model, creative incentives and employee recognition programs should be combined with efficient follow-up and individual performance reviews. This is not enough, however. It is also imperative that the institution stop tolerating or condoning corruption by particular staff members.

Several proposals have been made in recent years on ways to improve the delivery of health services, and various innovative approaches have been tried. These approaches attempted to combine new incentives for health care personnel with better services for beneficiaries. An experiment called Hospital Without Walls took place in San Ramón between 1971 and 1984. The experiment was based on a comprehensive community health care program and involved preventive care, educational services, and medical treatment. Although a complete evaluation of the program is not yet available, it is generally recognized that the model succeeded in attaining important coverage and impact goals. These achievements however, were not attained efficiently and cost-effectivly, thereby hampering any attempt to duplicate the experiment.

One of the most interesting experiments in the health sector probably relates to cooperative clinics. These are nongovernmental organizations that are contracted by CCSS to care for particular communities. Preliminary evaluations on the impact of these clinics have shown highly positive results, particularly in the area of meeting user needs. Results have also been acceptable in terms of costs, although definitive conclusions are yet to be drawn (Herrero and Villalta, 1992).

Funding and Budgets of Health Programs

Despite its successes and ability to overcome the challenges of the crisis, Costa Rica's health system has faced serious financial problems in recent years as a result of the lack of economic growth and an increasing concern over fiscal priorities.

The main challenge in health care disbursements is finding a more rational balance between medical treatment and preventive care. As for revenues, both the state and the private sector should make every effort to settle their debt with the Social Security Fund and to institute necessary rules and programs that would prevent these problems from recurring and would guarantee an equitable system.

It also seems advisable to institute user fees through the adoption of an innovative approach that, unlike what is usually suggested, would not require increasing fees for the more sophisticated services and for personal care (such as transplants, intensive care treatment, and high-risk surgery) or subsidizing basic medical services for the poor. Such steps would be less than evenhanded and would support the notion that health is essentially an asset of the private sector and not—as it has come to be defined in Costa Rica—a public asset. Rather, the intent is to provide two alternatives for health services: in one case, the fund's medical services would be offered as a "luxury" package, with charges reflecting costs; in the other case, the fund would offer the same medical services of identical quality but not with the same frills and not require additional fees above premium charges. This would integrate the current scheme of pensions and *biombos* into standard institutional procedures—not to the detriment of the insured or the institution but in their favor. This would also provide better arrangements for doctors in terms of transparency and legal incentives.

All of these reforms—from the reestablishment of an integrated vision within the health care system to implementing adequate cost recovery procedures—take into account the achievements and limitations of the Costa Rican health care system, which, for the most part, has had highly positive results. The system's outreach and progressiveness are encouraging. The constant pressure by its administrators for broader coverage, increasingly higher levels of quality, and more accessible services to the population's poorest sectors (such as has occurred in the recent liver and heart transplants) are reasons to be optimistic that problems will be corrected without having to abandon or sacrifice the system's markedly cohesive nature. Financial viability also seems to be attainable without having to abandon the system's basic principle of solidarity. However, this will require redefining practices in resource policy, management, and administration.

Education Services

Institutional Structure of Education Services

Since the last century, the Costa Rican government has been deeply involved in fostering education. In the 1800s it created schools, colleges, and a university; established free, compulsory elementary education; and hired European teachers. However, it was not until 1940, the year in which social policy as it is now known was established, that significant progress began to be made in raising the levels of quality, funding, and coverage in public education.

Education is under the supervision of the Ministry of Education. The ministry works through its own administrative structures and through the Superior Council on Education, an advisory entity. The ministry is responsible for creating guidelines and implementing education programs at the pre-school, elementary, and secondary levels. The ministry's main tasks include development of curricula and textbooks, evaluation of programs, teacher training, planning, and direct provision of education services.

Of the country's educational facilities, 91 percent are public, 8 percent are private, and 1 percent belong to semi-public colleges that are jointly managed by state and private entities. Pre-school, elementary, and secondary education are made available in 17 regions, each under the supervision of a center whose director has authority over the educational facilities located within the region. Each region has between five and 12 districts with about 20 educational facilities in each. The districts are coordinated by supervisors, and each facility has a board consisting of a chairman, parents, and community members, which provides guidance, supervises expenditures, and raises additional funds (Lynch, 1988; World Bank, 1991).

Higher education is divided into technical training and university studies. The former is offered by three state colleges, one semi-public institute, and 12 private institutes, and the latter, by four state and 10 private universities. Unlike institutions at the lower levels, state universities enjoy legal and administrative autonomy. Coordination among universities is carried out through the National Council of Deans, and coordination with government agencies, through the Joint Committee. The committee is made up of university deans and the ministers of finance, planning, science, and education, and is the forum in which university budgets are negotiated (Office of Planning for Higher Education, 1990).

Coverage and Impact of Public Spending on Education
Pre-school, Elementary, and Secondary Education

Costa Rica's achievements in public education at the pre-school, elementary, and secondary levels were, by the end of the 1970s, the fruit of a 30-year old policy of sustained support for the sector. While only half of elementary school teachers had completed elementary school in 1950, by the late 1980s, 90 percent had university degrees (Hidalgo and Monge, 1989). The country's literacy rate increased from 73 percent in 1940 to 94 percent by the end of the 1970s; coverage in elementary education rose from 68 percent to 101 percent during that same period; and for secondary education, it reached 60 percent.[3]

The impact of the 1980s economic crisis and the resulting stabilization and adjustment policies caused the only sustained lapse in spending on public preschool, elementary, and secondary education during the past four decades. Between 1981 and 1991, spending on education dropped from 20 percent to 14 percent of public spending, and from 4 percent to 3 percent of GDP. Real spending on education was slashed almost in half between 1980 and 1984, and

---

[3] Unless otherwise indicated, the indicators for pre-school, elementary, and secondary education were provided by the Ministry of Public Education (MEP), Office of Statistics. Figures for public spending were provided by Coto (1992).

Table 3.6. Public Education Spending, 1991
(percent)

	Primary and secondary education	Higher education	Total
Total[1]	18,880	10,748	29,628
Current expenditures	98.1	94.8	96.9
Wages and salaries	89.8	75.7	84.7
Others	6.7	10.7	8.2
Private sector transfers	1.6	8.4	4.1
Capital expenditures	1.9	4.8	3.0
Net loans granted	0.0	0.3	0.1

Source: Coto (1992).
Note: [1] In thousands of current colones.

although spending rates began to recover that year, they were still well below the level attained in early 1980. Real spending per registered student also dropped significantly, amounting in 1991 to only 78 percent of the level attained in 1980.

In addition to the severe public sector fiscal problems, education at the lower levels also lost somewhat in political importance. This is reflected in the different ways public and private education spending evolved. Although state spending fell considerably between 1981 and 1982, by the end of the decade it had recovered the GDP level attained in 1980, which, as we have seen, lower and secondary education spending failed to do.

One of the items most seriously affected by reduced spending on public education was capital spending, which was already relatively insignificant before the crisis. Between 1980 and 1991, the portion of capital spending on lower education dropped from 5 percent to 2 percent (see Table 3.6 for 1991's figures). This makes it increasingly difficult to maintain and repair deteriorating school facilities and to make investments that are necessary to satisfy increased demand for services or to improve the quality of education services. In 1991, the greater part of education spending was concentrated on elementary education, which received 60 percent of the spending. Secondary education received 34 percent, and pre-school 6 percent. However, per-student spending was 2.25 times greater in secondary education than total average spending at the elementary and pre-school levels.

Funding for public pre-school, elementary, and secondary depends entirely on the national budget and does not rely on earmarked fiscal revenues. Thus it was easy for the state to reduce its contributions to the sector during the crisis in the early 1980s, and to postpone significant increases in spending levels during

Table 3.7. Gross Enrollment in Public Education, Selected Years
(percent)

	1970	1975	1980	1984	1991
Lower education	74	81	81	74	81
Pre-school	13	27	39	44	68
Elementary	113	112	105	97	104
Cycle I	132	123	114	108	117
Cycle II	93	102	96	85	91
Secondary	35	53	61	52	52
Cycle III	44	62	68	56	60
Cycle IV	21	38	49	46	39
Higher education	6	12	15	15	16

Source: Ministry of Public Education Department of Statistics. CELADE.

the adjustment years. This contrasts, as we saw, with what occurred in the financing of the health sector, which—thanks to its three sources of financing—began a sustained recovery from the spending decline caused by the crisis that began in 1982.

Despite these financial problems, coverage for pre-school, elementary, and secondary education remained steady at levels held before the 1980s. As can be seen in Table 3.7, by 1991 the rate of gross enrollment equaled that of 1980. Also, net enrollment recovered from the 1980s decline, reaching 61 percent, the level it held in 1973. However, coverage by educational level exhibited significant variations. Gross enrollment for pre-school rose from 39 percent to 68 percent between 1980 and 1991, elementary enrollment remained stable at 104 percent, and secondary enrollment dropped from 61 percent to 52 percent, thus emerging as one of Costa Rica's primary problems in education. There were no significant changes in regional distribution since the difference in enrollment between urban and rural zones was the same in 1991 as it was in 1973, when rural net enrollment was 80 percent of urban enrollment.

Privately sponsored pre-school, elementary, and secondary education services, which make up 8 percent of the educational centers, account for 6 percent of total enrollment. Private coverage is largest at the pre-school level, representing 11 percent of total enrollment. In general, the population's higher-income sector prefers access to private schools and colleges. The cost of these institutions rose quite rapidly throughout the 1980s because of the deterioration in public education. This gave rise to a new type of institution that, unlike the traditional, nonprofit school, is strictly a profit-oriented business.

The relatively exclusive character of private education contrasts sharply with the progressive nature of public education. As can be seen in Table 3.8, the poor-

Table 3.8. Distribution of Elementary and Secondary Education Subsidies, 1986
(percent)

Quintile[1]	Elementary	Secondary
I	30	18
II	27	21
III	22	23
IV	13	21
V	8	17

Source: Sauma and Trejos (1990).
Note: [1] Quintile I represents the lowest level of income; quintile V, the highest.

est 40 percent of the population receives 57 percent of public spending, while the richest 40 percent receives only 21 percent. Spending at the secondary level is only slightly progressive, since the portion of the spending that the poorest 40 percent receive is only slightly higher than that of the richest 40 percent. Despite the decline in public education spending at the lower levels in the 1980s, allocations for that sector managed to maintain levels of coverage and progressive distribution since most allocations continued to be targeted to the poorest groups.

However, as can be seen in Table 3.9, increased deterioration in education services at the lower levels became unavoidable. This deterioration was characterized by, among other things, a reemergence of unqualified teachers who today make up more than 20 percent of elementary and secondary teaching staffs; an alarming reduction in the number of school days, which decreased by 22 percent between 1979 and 1990; inadequate maintenance of educational facilities to the extent that today 25 percent of classrooms are in urgent need of repair; a rising shortage of school materials whereby in 1991, 45 percent of elementary students had no textbooks; and the continued use of one-room schools, which still provide services for 10 percent of the country's students.

Higher Education

Enrollment in public higher education quadrupled during the 1970s. A policy of curriculum diversification led to the emergence of public junior colleges, various new professional training programs, and several private universities. Unlike what occurred at the lower levels, higher education survived the crisis of the 1980s without a decrease in financial support. Spending on higher education maintained its proportion of government spending and total GDP, accounting for 9 percent and 2 percent, respectively. Total real spending and real per capita spending did not change significantly either.

Coverage in higher education grew slightly in the last 10 years, as gross enrollment—which increased from 6 percent to 15 percent during the previous

Table 3.9. Data on Elementary Education

Percentage of unqualified elementary school teachers (1989)	23
Percentage of unqualified secondary school teachers (1989)	21
Total number of days in the school year (1990)	167
Reduction of the number of days in the school year (1979-90)	22
Percentage of schools with two shifts (1991)	98
Percentage of total elementary school registration in schools with only one teacher (1991)	9
Percentage of elementary school classrooms in urgent need of repair (1991)	25
Percentage of elementary school students with no textbooks (1991)	45
Percentage of students who passed standardized ministerial tests (1986):	
Mathematics, 6th year	37
Spanish, 6th year	16
Mathematics, 11th year	2
Spanish, 11th year	5

Source: Ministry of Education, Office of Statistics and Planning. World Bank (1991).

decade—rose to 16 percent in 1991 (Table 3.7). Besides stable financial allocations, another factor that contributed to this growth was the slow increase in demand for public higher education linked to demographic factors and increased availability of private service alternatives.[4] By 1991, private institutions accounted for 24 percent of university and 74 percent of junior college enrollments. The major changes in university enrollment, which in 1991 represented 88 percent of all enrollments in higher education, can explain the evolution in enrollment in private institutions. While state university enrollments increased at an average annual rate of 21 percent from 1971 to 1975, the average annual increase for 1981 to 1990 was barely 1 percent. This figure is considerably lower than the annual 15 percent increase for private university enrollment in the latter

---

[4] Unless otherwise indicated, the indicators for higher education are provided by the Office of Planning for Higher Education (1991).

years. It should be pointed out that while enrollment in state universities has grown slowly, the ratio of admissions to applications has increased. Thus, while half of those who applied between 1970 and 1975 were admitted, in 1990 and 1991 more than three quarters were admitted, a clear indication of lowered standards in state universitires.

State allocations to public universities have helped universities maintain their coverage in higher education and have brought about the decline in admission standards. Allocations from the national budget provide almost all of the universities' financial resources. Unlike schools at the lower level, universities operate with budgets that are guaranteed by the constitution. The political influence of the university community has also been vital in preserving current funding levels.

In terms of distribution, public higher education shows clear signs of regression. It is estimated that in 1986 the richest 20 percent of the country's families received 43 percent of higher education subsidies, while the poorest 20 percent received only 10 percent. Although regression does not seem to have worsened as a result of the economic crisis and the adjustment process (this situation is similar to what prevailed in 1977), regression is one of the main criticisms leveled against public spending in higher education (Sauma and Trejos, 1990). The problem does not lie with universities but with inequalities in society, in particular with inequalities in access by social classes to different levels of education and schools of different quality. The problem has been worsened by excessively lax tuition policies that end up subsidizing higher-income sectors.

Problems of the Education Sector

The main problem facing Costa Rica's education sector is not related to the structure, funding, or distribution issues that have already been discussed. Rather the problem lies with the quality of education and its impact on development. Over the past 20 years, Costa Rica lost, or did not develop, a capacity to enrich or energize human resources at its lower education levels. The country has not stimulated a culture that promotes effort, creativity, personal responsibility, and team work. Inferior quality is linked to a lack of qualified teachers, to inadequate training and motivation, and to the low quality and number of young people who aspire to become teachers. All of this is clearly reflected in the results of the national tests administered by the ministry in 1986 at the third and fourth cycles. An extremely low percent of students passed these tests satisfactorily (refer again Table 3.9). Higher levels of education attained even worse results.

Because education coverage has remained unchanged, it is clear that financial constraints are to blame for the deterioration in facilities and teacher working conditions, and that they have had an impact on the quality of education provided. This situation has been aggravated by the fact that the education sector has not been able to define a strategy, set program priorities, and allocate resources based on these priorities. Shifting attention from resource allocation to resource use, we also note that administrative practices have impeded the efficient use of allocated resources.

At the root of these problems appear to be the excessive responsibilities assigned to the ministry, responsibilities that the ministry has not always properly discharged. Its dual role as overseer and implementer of education policy has adversely affected the ministry's capacity and freedom to address important issues and has caused an excessive bureaucracy at all operating levels. As a result, the lack of a new management plan and strategic direction is more apparent in the education sector than in the health sector. The former does not have mechanisms for translating policy into operating decisions nor, much less, for implementing radical reassignment of resources. Administrative procedures are excessively rigid and inefficient, and the sector lacks qualified personnel for carrying out managerial tasks. User and community participation in education is minimal, as is the influence of local and regional authorities. Thus the system fails at its two extremes: neither central nor regional authorities have the capacity or the means to guide and make efficient use of the sector's allocated resources. A reduction in available resources would have had, however, the same results: loss of purpose, inferior quality, and setbacks in progressive spending. A great disparity exists at the lower levels of education. On the one hand there is the costly but superior private education, and on the other, the accessible but mediocre public education.

The paradox is that although higher education has been less affected financially by the crisis and adjustment process, it has not been able to use resources so as to satisfy its basic needs and reach the superior quality required for national development. Particularly evident is the deterioration in the quality of teaching staffs and in levels of activity. As at the lower levels, capital spending on higher education is quite low, reaching in 1991 only 5 percent of total spending. Failure to establish priorities has also aggravated this situation, as evidenced by excessive administrative costs, diminished spending on research, an abundance of unemployable graduates, and over-enrollments that have reduced the academic quality of education. Reduced availability of financial resources has led to the institution of tuition fees. These cover only a small fraction of costs, even though many of the students' families could afford higher tuitions.

Problems in the quality of higher education relate mainly to human resources. Inferior teaching staffs are the result of a relative deterioration in real wages, the inability of educational institutions to attract and keep qualified personnel, and weakened scholarship programs. Shortcomings in teacher training also affect this situation. The inequality resulting from the coexistence of two different work regimes is serious. On one side are the part-time teachers who lack job security and receive much lower wages; on the other are the career teachers who have stable jobs. Their jobs involve routine and undiversified work, thereby providing little incentive for professional development and limiting the possibility of staff turnovers when curricula changes are desirable. Administrative positions are characterized by low levels of performance and by work procedures that do not meet targeted objectives.

Private schools, which, for the most part, have evolved more as businesses than nonprofit educational institutions, are characterized by serious problems in quality. Inadequate information has left applicants unprotected and without means for evaluating their educational options, clearly a cost for society.

As a result, higher education has not been instrumental in encouraging development because of problems in both the quality and direction of education, and the efficiency and equity of allocated budgets. In developed countries, universities provide a significant part of the knowledge needed to spur the economy. In Costa Rica, university learning and the demands of the workplace are worlds apart. Many careers lag behind in terms of world knowledge, and graduates are not always properly trained to participate creatively in the development of the economy and national culture. This gap is widening rapidly since global scientific changes make careers and research centers become obsolete faster. Higher education must, therefore, recover its past role of social mobilizer by which it was, in the decades before the crisis, one of the most powerful elements in the modernization and social development of the country.

Challenges in the Education Sector

The Direction for Change

Education should fulfill three important tasks in the future development of Costa Rica. First, it must create the productive capacity needed to integrate the country into the international economy. Second, it must train individuals to exercise real freedom: the freedom to live as members of society. And, third, it must become one of the key instruments for motivating and integrating society.

As the World Bank is well aware, the countries that have been most successful in the war against poverty are precisely those that have advocated a growth model that includes the efficient use of human resources and have invested in the human capital of the poor (World Bank, 1990a, p. 57). As a result, a basic aspect of the reform in education is to develop in Costa Ricans the ability to "know how to work." This requires, of course, that companies learn how to invest in those productive activities that truly make the most of that teaching. An educational reform that maximizes the productive capacity of Costa Ricans is essential; however, it alone is not enough. Education must also develop the citizens' ability to "know how to live," which is equally important for the development of a democratic society and a free market. Uninformed and poorly educated consumers are not equipped to make decisions, to choose freely and wisely how to spend their income and how they want societies' resources to be invested. The more educated the society is, the greater the capacity of its citizens to face with real freedom the many choices offered by community life, from the trivial decisions on everyday consumption to more profound human choices. Finally, education fosters the integration and mobility of society's different members and sectors, which has traditionally been the case in Costa Rica. In fact, an essential feature that distinguishes Costa Rican history from that of its neighbors has been, precisely, the capacity to integrate, which allows Costa Ricans to appreciate belonging to a society that, despite its limitations, offers possibilities for growth and prosperity based on personal and collective efforts and incentives. The reform should restore to education its mission to develop that capacity for "knowing how to live together" that underlies the success of any democratic initiative.

The Strategy for Change

Costa Rica's educational reform should be based on principles of solidarity. Because of the macroeconomic pressures the country is enduring, the problems with education must be solved by redefining education strategies rather than through financial means. While the long-term goal is improvement of all public education, the first step should be to guarantee at least a core of first-rate public facilities. In this way, all young people who have the ability and are willing to make the effort will have access to a first-class education, regardless of their socioeconomic background. The project establishing colleges of science was conceived with this purpose in mind, and, in 1989, two excellent public colleges specializing in natural sciences were founded.

Further progress in this direction hinges on whether the ministry can effectively supervise the sector. Unlike the health sector, where the Ministry of Health's problems stem from its weakness vis-à-vis the Social Security Fund, the problems of the Ministry of Education stem from excessive responsibilities. The Ministry of Education should not have to deal with the implementation and administration of education programs. Rather it should concentrate its efforts on defining sectoral policies, formulating broad guidelines, and evaluating results. The Minister of Education should be an education strategist and not merely a school administrator or employer of teachers. Administration and teaching need to be decentralized and distributed in order to strengthen the ministry's role as overseer and to increase the power of agencies closest to users. It is not simply a question of transferring administrative responsibilities to municipalities or the private sector, but of achieving a more efficient public education program. A new management plan is needed to allow strategic, flexible, and transparent administration of education programs. In order for decision processes to bring about desired reassignments in resources, flexibility must be supplemented by adequate means of evaluation by both political authorities and the community.

Even with reform, financial constraints will continue to foment the unavoidable dilemma between preserving and increasing coverage in education and the need to improve education quality. The current education system makes it difficult to resolve this dilemma. Technological training for management, administration, and teaching personnel is an indispensable condition for improving the quality of education without sacrificing coverage. Information technology, audiovisual systems, and new education techniques help bridge the gap between mass education and quality education. The Education Information Program, which in five years has been introduced into 25 percent of the country's schools—beginning with those in the poorest communities—is a successful initiative contributing to the improvement of quality in education. This initiative was made possible thanks to a joint effort by a nongovernmental organization, the state, and communities.

As for financing, it should be obvious that any inclination to reduce budgets of lower education need to be resisted. In these financially depressed times, priorities should prevail, and funding for education should be a primary priority. Resources earmarked for education, though hopelessly insufficient, should be allocated and used with utmost efficiency. Education should be able to have access to the most efficient combination of private and public funding. Public financing will continue to underpin education policy since it provides access for most Costa Ricans to a range of quality services in education. The best use of the current mixed system under the education reform would be for private and public financial contributions to supplement each other, with every attempt being made to preserve the current equitable and unified character of the system.

Finally, teachers should be at the center of lower education reform. Thus, it is important that they be respected, receive higher salaries, and participate in radically revised and ongoing training processes. It would also be advisable to create a new system of specific incentives that benefit teachers who enroll in periodic professional enrichment courses.

Reform in Higher Education

Given the autonomy of state universities and the fast-paced growth of private universities, it would seem necessary to create an entity that would control the quality of training offered by these institutions, and implement procedures that would make available additional funds based on fulfillment of national goals. Such steps would redress some of the problems affecting higher education. They would restore to higher education its role in promoting development, particularly in the areas of production and social changes that are necessary ingredients of an open economy.

State institutions of higher learning need to become increasingly self-sufficient. They should supplement the public funds they receive by gradually raising tuition fees, taking into consideration the students' socioeconomic backgrounds. These revenues could be used primarily to finance scholarship programs for low-income students. The universities' link with productive sectors could also turn into an important source of additional funding but would require, in addition to legal and administrative changes, a cultural change within the institutions of higher learning.

These reforms should be spearheaded by teachers. For this purpose, work conditions should be standardized by eliminating existing inequalities among teachers; incentives be introduced that encourage efficiency and quality performance based on periodic evaluations; a remuneration policy be implemented that links wage increases to performance; and strong scholarship and post-graduate training programs be created.

As with the health care sector, these reforms consider not only the limitations of the education system but also its achievements. The reforms intend to rely on the sector's acquired experience, existing infrastructure, and institutional network to overcome the problems of the system. Improving the quality of public pre-school, elementary, and secondary education is, for Costa Rica, the most socially acceptable and cost-effective way to restore to education its dual role as promoter of economic and social development. Restoring a progressive and cohesive character to universal spending in education will further enhance the contribution of education to the social and political harmony that has come to characterize the country.

Social Welfare Services

In Costa Rica, universal programs in general education and health care are supplemented by a group of programs that target low-income groups. These programs, which aim to increase social equity and efficiency in public spending, have been considerably strengthened since December 1974 by the enactment of the law that created the Fund for Social Development and Family Allowance (FODESAF).

The purpose of this section is to analyze four FODESAF programs, two involving subsidies in kind and two involving cash subsidies for the indigent. These programs accounted for about 80 percent of total FODESAF resources and, in 1991, they collectively accounted for approximately $67 million. The

sum represented 3 percent of the consolidated spending of the nonfinancial public sector for that year, about 7 percent of public social spending, and around 1
percent of the country's GDP.

Institutional Structure of Social Welfare Services

The FODESAF was created to provide assistance to low-income Costa Ricans.
Its creation predates by more than a decade the Social Emergency Funds (FES)
and the Social Investment Funds (FIS) promoted by such organizations as the
World Bank. However, it is worth noting several basic factors that distinguish
the FODESAF funds.[5] The FODESAF is funded through earmarked taxes. The
funding level is, therefore, relatively stable over time and does not compete with
resources allocated to comprehensive programs. Thus, FODESAF funds are not
derived from ordinary budget allocations, which, to a large extent, are dependent
on periodic fiscal priorities, nor do they depend on extraordinary allocations,
which tend to be uncertain and increasingly controversial. An example of the latter allocations are the foreign assistance funds that finance the current FIS and
FES programs and that represent one of their main drawbacks.

The FODESAF accounts for about 1.5 percent of GDP. Thus, in its 15 years
of operation (1975-91), the fund has financed almost $1 billion of programs in
primary health care, food assistance, rural aqueducts, pensions for indigents,
and, more recently, direct housing subsidies.

The FODESAF channels resources to existing institutions, helping some
programs that are already operational and financing new ones. To qualify for
assistance, institutions need to have an effective operational program. This
avoids duplication of administrative efforts and waste associated with a public
social infrastructure that the state cannot run or service adequately.

The FODESAF is a permanent organization whose mission is to finance
programs that provide direct assistance to training and to enhancement of education-related resources at an early stage, thus increasing their long-term potential.
This program reinforces existing comprehensive programs by complementing
their efforts. It should be pointed out that this permanent character is already present in the current FIS, which were established as temporary assistance activities
within the framework of adjustment programs and have evolved in permanent
social programs. An example of such an evolution is Bolivia's Social Emergency
Fund, which became the Social Investment Fund. The underlying notion of per-

---

5 Bolivia's Social Emergency Fund is usually considered to be the first of such initiatives. It
was created in 1987 and was later duplicated in other countries of the region. Although some
authors such as Franco, Cohen and Rufán (1991) recognize the prior initiatives as being highly
significant, they tend to ignore the existence of the FODESAF.

manence can also be observed in funds that have recently been established in various Latin American countries, such as the Venezuelan Social Investment Fund (FONVIS), Chile's Solidarity and Social Investment Fund (FOSIS), Peru's National Compensation and Social Development Fund (FCS), Guatemala's Social Investment Fund (FIS), and Ecuador's Social Investment Fund (FISE) (Martínez and Wurgaft, 1992).

Finally, the FODESAF does not operate at the periphery of existing legislation, but abides by norms that regulate public administration related to resource management, personnel hiring, and remuneration. Although abiding by these norms has deprived the fund of a certain degree of flexibility, in practice it has not hampered its operations. This suggests that the fund's structure need not be unique since demands for a unique structure would tend to inhibit efforts for achieving an effective institutional reform.

The General Office of Social Development and Family Allowances (DESAF), a decentralized entity under the Ministry of Labor, is responsible for the general administration of the FODESAF. The DESAF, together with the Ministry of Planning, annually approves programs for funding. Applicants must present proposals requesting FODESAF contributions to supplement their own. Fiscal responsibilities related to the use and disbursement of the DESAF funds lie with the General Comptroller of the Republic. This process is carried out in a relatively efficient manner, as reflected by the fact that the administrative costs of the fund—which include collection, administration, control and supervision—are quite low, and generally fall under 3 percent.

FODESAF resources fund more than 50 programs that can be grouped in five areas: (1) health, food, and nutrition; (2) housing; (3) development of production and employment activities; (4) training and professional formation; and (5) child, elderly, and family protection. The distribution of resources by area shows a certain degree of flexibility in adapting to particular economic trends. During the crisis of the early 1980s, coverage programs gained in importance, while health care and nutrition sector requirements declined because of systematic improvements achieved in these fields.

Table 3.10 illustrates the basic characteristics of the four social welfare programs. Food programs predate the FODESAF by many years. Creation of the FODESAF, however, strengthened and helped these programs significantly increase the number of beneficiaries (about 510 thousand individuals in 1991). Food program outlays are relatively small because of the limited amount of subsidies offered. However, the pre-school food program is costlier because it incorporates education and health services. The coverage of the fund's cash subsidy programs is limited and a heavier burden on available resources. In this regard, the housing subsidy also stands out, given the large allocations it requires, the appreciable volume of average annual subsidies it provides, and the broad network of intermediate private financial institutions it uses.

Table 3.10. General Features of the Social Welfare Programs, 1991

Feature	School lunch	Child care	Pension for indigents	Housing subsidy
Year started	1944	1951	1975	1987
Responsible	Ministry of Education	Ministry of Health	Costa Rican Social Security Fund	Home Mortgage Bank
Objective	To improve student nutritional status and education	To provide comprehensive care to children under 6 years of age and mothers	To transfer resources to seniors not covered by contributory system	To help poor families become homeowners
Type of service	Food and nutritional education	Food and nutritional pre-school education, medical care	Monthly monetary subsidy Medical care	Monetary subsidy to build or purchase housing; Supplementary credit
Target population	Elementary and secondary students in public education centers	Children 1-6 years of age from poor homes, with behav. problems or working mother. Poor women who are pregnant or nursing	Seniors over 64 years of age, indigent, invalid, widows, not covered by insurance, orphans under 15 years of age	Homeless families with an adjusted income of less than four construction worker minimum wages
Beneficiaries (No. of individuals)	452,217	57,867	73,233	65,130
Apparent coverage[1]	Elementary: 95% Secondary: 31%	Children: 57% Mothers: 23%	Seniors: 110%[2]	Families: 20%
Average subsidy (US$)	$22 per year	$272 per year	$167 per year	$2,916 per settlement

Source: Authors' calculations, based on information from the responsible institutions.
Notes: [1] Assuming there is no screening and as a percentage of the target population.
        [2] Compared to senior population of the poorest quintile.

Table 3.11. Features of the Focusing Mechanisms of the Social Welfare Programs, 1992

Feature	School lunch	Child care	Pension indigents	Housing subsidy
Focusing	Geographic	Nutritional risk questionnaire	Social worker evaluation	Questionnaire
Type of administration	Centralized	Decentralized	Decentralized	Decentralized
Facilities and networks	DANEA[1]	577 centers 541 health posts 9 Regional	5 regional 69 branches	6 mutuals 25 cooperatives 3 NGOs 3 Public Institutions
Private sector participation	Student sponsorship	Nutritional committee	None	Financial institutions and construction companies
Advantages	Simplicity Low cost	Verifiable objective	Can identify special situations	Simplicity
Disadvantages	Imprecision	A posteriori action	No uniform criteria Client-based	Imprecision Strong incentive to provide inaccurate information
Beneficiaries among the poorest 40%	62.0%	76.3%	64.3%	71.0%
Overall progressivity[2]	-0.2868	-0.4768	-0.3204	-0.4276

Source: Authors' calculations based on information from the responsible institutions.
Notes: [1] Student and Adolescent Nutrition Division (Ministry of Education).
        [2] Gini coefficient of the distribution of beneficiaries by quintile (the closer to -1 the more low-income segments are benefited).

Coverage and Impact of the FODESAF Programs

Targeting and Equity

The FODESAF was created to channel resources to low-income groups and, thus, to supplement universal social policies. For this reason, programs financed by the Fund should be tailored to the needs of these groups and should incorporate mechanisms that allow appropriate selection of the groups.

Table 3.11 displays the main characteristics and results of the selection mechanisms that were implemented. The Child Care Program shows the greatest targeting thanks to a particularly decentralized mechanism, with more than 75 percent of beneficiaries belonging to the poorest 40 percent of the population.

Part of the program's success is due to the use of verifiable, objective criteria such as malnutrition, although these criteria imply using specialists and, therefore, costly personnel. The Housing Subsidy Program is next in importance in terms of targeting, despite the fact that the subsidy, either in whole or in part, is available to 80 percent of the country's families and that the selection process is carried out by private financing entities. Even so, more than 70 percent of its beneficiaries come from the poorest 40 percent of the population.[6]

The other two programs, though less successful, also maintained appreciable levels of targeting. In the School Lunch Program, 62 percent of beneficiaries belong to the poorest 40 percent of families. The reason for this is that in its early days the program had a universal outlook and that, despite the recent introduction of geographic targeting criteria that set up three levels of priorities, the reassigned subsidies are still being distributed among the same beneficiaries. The Pension Program for Indigents lacks targeting given the type of subsidy and the target population involved, with the result that less than 60 percent of the users are among the poorest 40 percent of the population. Even though the process is carried out entirely by professionals, the lack of concrete criteria and of a standard methodology for identifying beneficiaries, as well as the presence of political pressures affecting the grant of benefits, explain the poor targeting results.

Table 3.12 presents an overview on the level of equity for programs and indicates beneficiary and subsidy participation by quintiles of per capita family income. Two additional estimates on subsidy distribution have been incorporated in the table: in the case of school lunches, a hypothetical subsidy distribution based on the premise of an exact relation between geographic targeting criteria and income quintiles; and in the case of housing subsidies, a subsidy distribution based on income levels.

The first case shows how, in programs of widespread coverage, the level of equity can be significantly increased by using schemes that involve well differentiated average subsidies. The second case shows how targeting can also be improved if differential subsidy schemes based on income levels are incorporated into the careful targeting of the target population. The table also includes an approximation of the incidence of funding. The FODESAF's and the government's budgets rely largely on indirect taxes for their revenues. Therefore, the distribution of total household expenditures is a good approximation of the distribution of financial contributions to these programs. The latter distribution shows an inverse relation to the programs studied. Thus it is expected that the net

---

6 The data of this program should be analyzed with caution. Because the program has not been in operation long, there is no independent survey information that allows verification of household-supplied information and evaluation of institution selection criteria. Thus, the targeting of the data has an upper limit.

Table 3.12. Distribution of Beneficiaries and Subsidies by Income Level
(percent)

| | Quintiles of per capita income[1] | | | | | | Overall |
	I	II	III	IV	V	Total	Progressivity[2]
School lunches (1986)							
Beneficiaries	33.2	28.8	20.3	11.9	5.8	100.0	-0.287
Subsidy[3]	51.5	22.9	13.6	8.1	3.9	100.0	-0.440
Child care centers (1982-86)							
Beneficiaries	52.9	23.4	14.4	8.6	0.7	100.0	-0.477
Pensions for indigents (1986)							
Beneficiaries	42.3	22.0	15.0	14.9	5.8	100.0	-0.320
Housing subsidies (1988-91)							
Beneficiaries	49.7	21.3	15.7	12.8	0.5	100.0	-0.428
Subsidy[4]	53.7	21.9	14.3	9.8	0.3	100.0	-0.477
Program financing (1988)							
Taxpayers	7.2	12.7	16.2	21.6	42.3	100.0	0.316

Source: Sauma and Trejos (1990) and Trejos (1992).
Notes: [1] Quintile I represents the lowest level of income; quintile V, the highest.
 [2] Gini coefficient of the distribution of the subsidy and total household spending (taxpayers). For the former, the closer the coefficient is to -1 the more low-income segments are benefited. For the latter, the closer to 1 the more the burden of financing falls on the high-income segments.
 [3] Hypothetical distribution assuming that the geographic selectivity corresponds to the per-capita income quintiles.
 [4] Hypothetical distribution assuming that the allocation of the subsidy, which decreases as per-capita family increases, corresponds exactly to the position of the families in the income quintiles.

subsidy will be, in all cases, more progressive. In short, although program targeting could be improved, it is still a valuable tool.

Funding

The FODESAF relies for its funding on a tax that is equivalent to 5 percent of the companies' and institutions' payrolls—a tax that the CCSS collects and transfers to the fund—and on a 20 percent assessment of general sales tax revenues. The latter assessment is collected and transferred to the fund by the Ministry of Finance.

While specific-purpose taxes introduce inflexibilities in budget administration, they reduce, on the other hand, the vulnerability of these programs to fiscal constraints. However, such an arrangement does not entirely eliminate vulnerability since the government, through budget modifications, has occasionally changed the percent allocated to the fund. Although revenues acquired by taxing payrolls have accounted for an average 61 percent of FODESAF's ordinary funds in the last decade, this figure has fluctuated between 50 percent and 74 percent. The vulnerability has also been evidenced by the fact that in the last four years the Ministry of Finance has not transferred the operating expenses owed to the fund, averaging 25 percent, and has not implemented 37 percent of planned spending.

Another inherent problem of FODESAF's funding scheme is its cyclical character, which reduces the fund's ability to react in recessionary periods, that is, precisely at times when it can have the greatest impact and when its need is greatest. As can be seen in Table 3.13, after a strong expansion in the second half of the 1970s, the fund's resources contracted substantially in the first half of the 1980s, a period characterized by widespread recession and extreme poverty. During the following five years, the fund recovered economically only to shrink again at the beginning of the 1990s, when the Costa Rican economy once again faced a recession.[7]

Two additional problems need to be pointed out. The first relates to existing commitments that target fund resources to specific projects. This reduces flexibility in allocation of funds and in financing new programs. Specific allocations have generally been small. This, however, has not been the case for housing subsidies, which by law command 33 percent of the fund's resources and which have restricted the funding of other programs. The second significant shortcoming facing FODESAF, and in particular the DESAF, is the lack of clear follow-up, control, and evaluation mechanisms of fund-assisted programs. Therefore, once a program has been selected, it is difficult to suspend its financial support later.

The entitlement-based character of FODESAF resources causes programs it finances to mirror those of the fund as a whole. However, these programs present peculiarities that should be pointed out. On the one hand, the school lunch program—which relies almost exclusively on the fund for its financing and which does not have fixed allocations—was the one program most seriously affected by the real reduction of funds and could not recover during the second half of the 1980s. Program incomes in 1991 were less than half of those 12 years earlier. The lack of adequate resources is undoubtedly one of the program's major limitations, especially if one keeps in mind that the number of beneficiaries has not declined.

An opposite behavior is observed in the Child Care Program, which was able to maintain, and even increase, its real resources during the first half of the

---

7 Part of the economic expansion in the 1970s resulted from a gradual introduction of payroll taxes that initially were assessed at 2 percent and increased 1 percent per year until reaching the scheduled 5 percent.

Table 3.13. Trend of Real FODESAF Resources, 1975-91

Year	Total spending (1980=100)	FODESAF as a percent of		
		GDP	Public spending	Social spending
1975	34.9	1.0	2.7	5.1
1976	49.5	1.2	3.4	6.8
1977	69.4	1.4	3.6	8.1
1978	91.2	1.7	4.2	8.5
1979	93.7	1.7	3.9	7.3
1980	100.0	1.8	4.0	7.7
1981	84.3	1.5	3.9	8.7
1982	67.9	1.3	3.7	9.4
1983	80.1	1.6	3.8	10.1
1984	7.9	1.5	3.8	9.4
1985	98.1	1.6	4.1	10.0
1986	101.9	1.5	3.8	8.6
1987	107.5	1.6	4.4	9.4
1988	135.5	2.0	5.3	11.3
1989	100.2	1.4	3.6	7.4
1990	108.3	1.5	3.8	8.3
1991	93.4	1.3	3.5	7.6

Source: Office of the General Controller of the Republic, Central Bank and Ministry of Finance.

1980s because of the enactment of an import tax specifically designed to support it. However, in recent years, the program's resources have shrunk and, although the decline has not been as marked as that for the School Lunch Program, it has resulted in a significant reduction in effective coverage.

The Pension Program for Indigents relies on a fixed percent allocation by FODESAF, and thus its evolution is similar to that of the fund as a whole. Except for 1991, a year in which it faced a strong reduction in allocations, the program has managed to enjoy relatively stable levels of funding. Finally, the Housing Subsidy Program shows a more erratic evolution because it depends strongly on contributions from the national budget, a budget that has been constrained by fiscal discipline.

Efficiency

Aside from their dependence on FODESAF resources—with the possible exception of the Child Care and Housing Subsidy Programs—each program exhibits specific peculiarities and problems in its use of resources. This is shown in Table 3.14. The School Lunch Program problems relate to insufficient resources, high operational costs, and considerable targeting criteria. Because of inadequate resources, the program has lost its ability to improve the nutritional condition of students efficiently, a fact which has been worsened by the high proportion of the total budget allocated to salaries of cooking staffs. Thus, in 1991, out of $22 spent per student, only $13 represented food costs, that is, about eight cents per dollar per school day.[8] Selectivity considerations are important, although it should be noted that the program does not include criteria for excluding any prospective beneficiary.

While the Child Care Program shows appreciable degrees of targeting, it also suffers from limited coverage and high operational costs. The problem of coverage has deteriorated in recent years because of reductions in real resources. However, even in years when coverage was at its highest, it was not sufficient to take care of the entire target population. Coverage was unavailable for part of the pre-school population belonging to the first two quintiles.

The Pension Program for Indigents has limited coverage and many tiers of selectivity. Thus, what is necessary is the introduction of more efficient targeting mechanisms to increase coverage for the elderly population belonging to the poorest family quintile. The problem in this case is the insufficient subsidy granted to each beneficiary. This subsidy, at the outset of the program in 1975, was equivalent to 67 percent of the minimum salary of a farm worker. In 1991, this fraction was only 16 percent. Although the subsidy reduction can act as a self-targeting mechanism, it is, however, a detrimental one.

Finally, because it is financed by the national budget, the popular Housing Subsidy Program is somewhat vulnerable. For example, of the C3 billion allocated by law, only half was budgeted, and the program received only C250 million. In other words, it received a mere 8 percent of its entitlement. As a result, the reserve funds accumulated during the program's early years had to be tapped, and by 1991, 95 percent of those resources were used up. This means that from 1992 on, the program will be able to rely only on resources it can raise annually. It is not a coincidence that the revival of the previous reserve system is being considered to alleviate, over time, demands on the program. This, however, means excluding from the program precisely the poorest groups.

Problems and Challenges of Social Welfare Programs

The FODESAF has proven to be a powerful financing tool for selected social programs. It allows implementation of assistance policies and preservation of consistent macroeconomic equilibria. It represents, therefore, an experience that can be repeated in other countries. However, areas that will require attention include budget vulnerabilities, growing inflexibilities in resource allocation, and inadequate mechanisms for control.

---

8 Each school lunch room operates 160 days per year.

Instituting special purpose taxes for providing the fund with a fixed source of revenues has proven useful over time as a means to stabilize the fund's resources. However, the fund's current financial weakness results from a failure on the part of the Ministry of Finance to enforce this legislation.

The growing inflexibility in the allocation of fund resources is a problem that needs to be resolved. Only housing subsidies and pensions for indigents, which receive 53 percent of FODESAF's resources, are mandated by law. Whether the housing program should be entitled to such high allocations or whether its cost should be alleviated by additional contributions from the national budget and alternate sources of income should become an issue open to debate.

The lack of evaluation, control, and follow-up procedures for FODESAF-funded programs represents another of the system's significant shortcomings. Administrative budgets of the FODESAF could be increased. Such an increase, however, would be justified only if it brought about improvements in the fund's control and assessment of allocations. In this sense, it would be important to finance periodic surveys that measure accessibility and equity of different programs implemented throughout the country. Greater autonomy might also be granted to the DESAF, transforming this organization into an agency that operates separately from the Ministry of Labor.

Increased targeting, establishment of an integrated service system, and more efficient use of resources, should be program goals of the reform. While all programs could improve targeting, this aim should not be promoted at the expense of weakening the programs through lost political support, which clearly seems to have been the case with school lunches and housing subsidies. In the case of school lunches, the program relies on and fosters widespread community participation. Targeting, therefore, can be increased without reducing overall coverage by establishing a wide range of subsidies, as was done for housing subsidies, based on the type of school assisted. Setting priorities would require, however, evaluation of a new set of indicators.

A priority for the Pension Program for Indigents is increased targeting, which implies increased per capita subsidies. This program needs to be focused. The use of social workers is not only expensive, but also inefficient. Furthermore, the CCSS is not interested in continuing as manager of the program since it has required the agency to rely on nontransparent subsidies in the form of health services. Therefore, the CCSS has proposed that the program be transferred to the Ministry of Labor. Perhaps a more appropriate authority would be the Combined Institute of Social Health. The institute is now testing compilation of a single directory of beneficiaries classified and identified by socioeconomic criteria.

Child care centers provide an attractive range of services but are also well integrated into primary health care programs. It is estimated that the centers, on the whole, were responsible for about 40 percent of the remarkable decline in infant mortality registered during the 1970s (Rosero, 1985). These centers can enhance targeting by excluding children who require only child care services but who do not represent nutritional risks. The families of children at risk could rely on the recently established community houses for assistance.

It is evident from an evaluation of the School Lunch Program that the program is unable to provide the required nutritional assistance. Once again, this points out the need to increase the program's resources. Increasing the range of subsidies would require steps to reduce the target population and operational costs. The former objective may be attained without detriment to the community by eliminating lunch programs in secondary schools and expanding their scholarship programs. The latter objective may be attained by reducing costs by replacing cooking staffs with voluntary workers and by relying on contributions from the community.

Conclusions

Latin American countries are in the midst of an intense process aimed at redefining their relationships to the global economy. In this context, as was pointed out in a recent research paper on international competition (Porter, 1990; CEPAL, 1990 and 1992), the direct link between compensation of productive factors—work, in particular—and the efficiency with which these factors are used in production should become the centerpiece of an effective development policy. Only a sustained and effective effort to change over to deliberate and systematic forms of technical progress can allow and require an increasingly productive and highly remunerated use of the work force. This, in turn, constitutes "the main mechanism by which the large majorities can contribute and participate in the fruits of development" (CEPAL, 1992, p. 18).

To achieve these goals, social policy must guarantee access to services in education, health, housing, and environmental health. These services represent the fundamental building blocks that enhance the quality of life of workers and their families, as well as their productive capacity. However, extending coverage of these services is not by itself sufficient. It is necessary that these programs fit specific needs that arise when life and production styles change, and that the programs incorporate satisfactory quality levels. In particular, this presupposes achieving an adequate compromise between basic social service delivery and access to more specialized services. These services underpin both the quality of life and successful participation in the international economy.

These programs should constitute the core of a well-understood social policy that would allow Latin American countries to overcome the problem of increasing poverty. However, initiatives must not be limited only to the domain of these programs. In effect, both past constraints (which have impoverished over 50 percent of the population in many countries) and the current limitations (which combine the devastating effects of the economic crisis with the even worse economic impact of the adjustment process) require that social policy move well beyond these programs. According to the World Bank, even when basic strategies are successful, many of the poor continue to suffer serious deprivations. Thus, a widespread effort to reduce poverty requires that basic strategies be supplemented with transfers and safeguarding programs that target specific groups (World Bank, 1990a, p. 3).

The problem lies in how to deal with the challenges of both social development and social compensation at the same time. These two issues complement each other in an environment in which the critical state of public finances faces both a chronic deterioration of state institutions and social services and a growing demand for these services. This is particularly significant when one considers the role that public sector intervention has had in countries that have achieved the most significant improvements in social development. In Costa Rica, as the study has pointed out and the World Bank has acknowledged, we have seen that the public sector has had a pivotal role in promoting economic growth and, in particular, social development.[9]

Not only have countries like Costa Rica used their public sectors to offset weaknesses in their private sectors and to deal with decreases in revenues, but so have some of the countries with stronger private sectors and higher revenue flows. As Amartya Sen recently stated, "The point is that even for the cases of high growth performance coupled with substantial private sector success, one sees the fruitfulness of using growth-generated returns as a means for expanding social security and the quality of life through the public sector" (Sen, 1990, p. 422).

As we have also seen throughout this chapter, the problems and limitations that Costa Rica's state institutions face in providing services of acceptable coverage and quality, without excessively burdening fiscal equilibria, are real. The problems' severity is such that, if they are not resolved they will eventually destroy the whole framework of the country's successful social policy system. However, it is also true that these problems do not lessen the achievements attained by Costa Rica's social policy, by its institutions, and by a large segment of its civil servants. In this context, weighing both the positive and negative aspects of the Costa Rican system, there can be no room for solutions that simply

---

[9] According to the World Bank, the public sector has traditionally played a central role in Costa Rica. Led by the expansion of the basic infrastructure and a marked increase in social sector spending, GNP grew at an average annual rate of almost 6 percent during 1957-1980. At the same time, public education, health, and welfare programs in Costa Rica placed the country's social indicators among the highest in the Western Hemisphere (World Bank, 1989, p. 3).

propose transferring the administration of social services to the private sector and that see in the targeting of social policy, as a whole, as the only possible solution for Latin American countries.

Costa Rica's experience contradicts those who maintain that, in general, the effectiveness of social policies and institutions is questionable, since the policies and institutions have not been able to integrate the poorest groups into social service delivery networks even in countries where such policies and institutions are more developed. According to Infante, Matte, and Sancho (1992), the principal beneficiaries of social programs were the administrators themselves who "established powerful organizations that exerted pressures to gain access to the growing benefits of programs they themselves managed. As these programs grew and became costlier, benefits were extended to groups that were already in the system, thus making it increasingly more difficult to incorporate the poor (Infante *et al*, 1992, p. 32) In the opinion of these same authors, administrators "deliberately created restrictions that would hamper access to other social groups."

Clearly, there are situations in Latin America that justify, in certain cases, such statements. Despite the problems that have been pointed out, the Costa Rican case is a valid exception. The validity of the hypothesis that the problems pointed out by Infante, Matte, and Sancho are not inherent in state interventions that deliver social services is proven by the following considerations: the impact and progressive nature of the Costa Rican health care system; the insistence of administrators on continuously expanding coverage and their capacity to make even the most specialized treatment available to the population's poorest segments; the expansion of the education system and the high level of education for the population; the impact of professional training in the modernization of the country; the capacity to promote innovative and daring programs such as the Educational Information System; and the visionary nature of the Social Development and Family Allowances Fund. These considerations highlight the capacity of the country to use the instruments of social policy to reach quality of life levels that are substantially higher than those that their economic potential would seem to allow. As a matter of fact, experience suggests that without state intervention, Costa Rica would not have been able to achieve the levels of social development and the style of political harmony that it enjoys today.

This being the case, it seems much more reasonable to dedicate the greatest possible effort to face constructively the problems of the public health system, education, and social assistance and not to dismantle an institutional development, which, however limited, has shown itself to be indispensable for the achievements attained.

BIBLIOGRAPHY

Centro Latinoamericano de Demografía (CELADE). 1988. *Costa Rica: estimaciones y proyecciones de población (1950-2025)*. San José: CELADE.

Comisión Económica para América Latina (CEPAL). 1990. *Transformación productiva con equidad*. Santiago: United Nations.

————. 1992. *Equidad y transformación productiva: un enfoque integrado*. Santiago: United Nations.

Coto, M. 1992. *Estadísticas sobre el sector público consolidado: 1983-1991*. San José: Secretaría Técnica de la Comisión Bipartidista para la Reforma del Estado.

Franco, R., E. Cohen, and D. Rufián. 1991. Los fondos de desarrollo social. *Cuadernos de Ciencias Sociales* (No. 45).

Garnier, L. 1991. Gasto público y desarrollo social en Costa Rica. *Cuadernos de Política Económica* (No. 2).

Herrero, D., and O. Villalta. 1992. Informe comparativo sobre las clínicas de Tibás y Pavas y varias clínicas de la CCSS. San José, Costa Rica. Mimeo.

Hidalgo, R., and G. Monge. 1989. *El futuro cercano y la capacidad tecnológica costarricense*. San José: EUNED/Editorial de la Universidad de Costa Rica.

Infante, T., P. Matte, and A. Sancho. 1992. Reforma de los sistemas de prestación de servicios sociales en América Latina. Inter-American Development Bank, Washington, D.C., Mimeo.

Kleysen, B. 1988. *Private Expenditures on Health Care*. San José: Instituto de Investigaciones en Ciencias Económicas.

Lynch, P. 1988. *La organización de la educación general en Costa Rica*. San José: The World Bank/MIDEPLAN.

Martínez, D., and J. Wurgaft. 1992. Fondos de inversión social: situación y perspectivas. Paper presented at conference, El Seminario Final del Proyecto Regional Políticas para Pagar la Deuda Social. Viña del Mar, Chile. OIT-PREALC/PNUD.

Ministerio de Planificación Nacional y Política Económica (MIDEPLAN). 1992. *Programa nacional de reforma del sector salud.* San José: MIDE-PLAN.

Miranda, G. 1988. *La seguridad social y el desarrollo en Costa Rica.* San José: Editorial Nacional de Salud y Seguridad Social.

Office of Planning for Higher Education (Oficina de Planificación de la Educación Superior). 1990. *Posibilidades de estudio en la educación superior universitaria estatal de Costa Rica.* San José: CONARE.

―――. 1991. *Estadísticas de la educación superior 1979-1990.* San José: CONARE.

Porter, M. 1990. *The Competitive Advantage of Nations.* New York: The Free Press.

Rodríguez, A. 1986. *El gasto público en salud y su impacto en la distribución del ingreso familiar.* Working Document No. 100, Instituto de Investigaciones en Ciencias Económicas, San José, Costa Rica.

Rosero, L. 1985. Determinantes del descenso de la mortalidad en Costa Rica. In *Demografía y epidemiología en Costa Rica.* San José: Asociación Demográfica Costarricense.

Sáenz, L., and M. León. 1992. Gastos de los hogares en servicios de salud privados en Costa Rica durante 1987-1988. Ministry of Health, San José. Mimeo.

Sanguinetti, J. 1988. La salud y el seguro social en Costa Rica. Informe final del proyecto de asistencia técnica: Ministry of Planning. San José: The World Bank.

Sauma, P., and J.D. Trejos. 1990. *Evolución reciente de la distribución del ingreso en Costa Rica.* Working Document No. 132, Instituto de Investigaciones en Ciencias Económicas, University of Costa Rica, San José, Costa Rica.

Sen, A. 1990. Development Strategies: the Roles of the State and the Private Sector. In *Proceedings of the World Bank Annual Conference on Development Economics.* Washington, D.C.: The World Bank.

Trejos, J.D. 1992. Costa Rica: focalización y seguimiento de programas sociales en gran escala. Document prepared for CEPAL's Division of Social Development for the Third Regional Conference on Poverty in Latin America and the Caribbean. Santiago, Chile.

United Nations Development Program (UNDP). 1992. *Desarrollo humano: informe 1992*. Santafé de Bogotá: Tercer Mundo Editores.

The World Bank. 1989. *Costa Rica: Public Sector Expenditure Review.* Washington, D.C.: The World Bank.

————. 1990a. *Informe sobre el desarrollo mundial, 1990: la pobreza.* Washington, D.C.: The World Bank.

————. 1990b. *Costa Rica: el gasto público en los sectores sociales.* Report No. 8519CR. Washington, D.C.: The World Bank.

————. 1991. *Staff Appraisal Report. Basic Education Rehabilitation Project.* Washington, D.C.: The World Bank.

Weinstock, H., *et al.* 1992. La salud como parte de un nuevo esquema de desarrollo nacional: retos y alternativas. *Nuevo surco* (No. 1).

CHAPTER FOUR

SETTING A NEW AGENDA FOR
THE DOMINICAN REPUBLIC

Isidoro Santana and Magdalena Rathe*

The Dominican Republic's social and economic life is greatly affected by its proximity to Haiti, the most impoverished country in the Western Hemisphere. Haitian labor migration to the Dominican Republic strongly affects the country's social service delivery, as does the simultaneous migration of Dominican labor to developed countries. Thus, the country's human resources are continuously being supplanted by others who are less qualified and less productive.

The population of the Dominican Republic was estimated in 1992 at 7.5 million. With 154 people per square kilometer, the country has one of the highest population densities in Latin America. Total GDP for 1992 was estimated at $1,065 per capita, a relatively low figure for Latin America.[1]

Recent Economic Trends

The Dominican Republic's rapid economic growth and new industrialization in the 1970s were linked to global economic expansion. In the early 1980s, however, the country was forced to implement restrictive adjustment policies to offset the adverse impact of the debt crisis. Although these programs were designed to guarantee a viable economy attuned to international conditions, they caused a significant decline in per capita production and in public social spending, thus aggravating conditions in an already deteriorated social sector.

Following the early 1986 adjustment period, the government undertook an ambitious public investment program in public works and urban renewal in order to stimulate the economy. The program did not rely on foreign capital but

* The authors are grateful to Juan Ernesto Cabral, César Pérez, and Beatriz Henríquez for their collaboration and to Rosángela Sánchez and Tammy Pou for their editorial assistance. They also wish to thank the entire ECOCARIBE staff for their help.
[1] Amounts are in U.S. dollars unless otherwise noted.

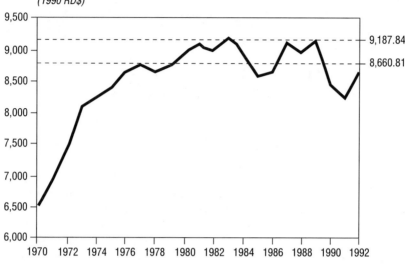

Figure 4.1. Per Capita Gross Domestic Product
(1990 RD$)

Source: ECOCARIBE, based on Central Bank data.

was financed through an increase in money supply. This worsened the country's external position and resulted in high inflation. Thus, the country again experienced a macroeconomic imbalance caused not by a struggle for social progress, but by the government's emphasis on public works.

A new economic adjustment program was implemented during the second half of 1990, and a stand-by agreement with the International Monetary Fund (IMF) was signed in 1991. The program quickly brought inflation under control and improved the economy's external position. However, it also brought about a significant reduction in real per capita GDP for two consecutive years (10 percent during 1989-91) and adversely affected employment and public social spending.

As can be seen in Figure 4.1, per capita GDP in 1991 was similar to the amount achieved two decades ago and was 11 percent lower than the maximum per capita value attained before the economic crisis. Greater stability in 1992 fostered economic recovery and brought about a 5 percent increase in per capita GDP. However, as Figure 4.1 shows, this increase hardly reached mid-1970 levels.

Along with its macroeconomic adjustment policy, the government has also undertaken an ambitious structural reform program involving tax and tariff regimes, methods of financing, and labor relations. The aim of the reform is to bring greater openness and transparency to interactions among economic agents, thereby strengthening the economic recovery.

Many of these reform measures are either under discussion, pending approval, or in the process of being implemented. Because of the progress achieved in economic reform, several business sectors are supporting the idea of a future reform to the state itself and a greater emphasis on social services.

Social Policy in the Dominican Republic

Income Distribution and Poverty

Social inequality is part of the country's historical legacy. Current data show that income distribution patterns have indeed worsened in recent years. The share of the poorest decile decreased from 2.1 percent in 1984 to only 0.8 percent in 1989. The share of the highest decile, however, rose from 33 percent in 1984 to 44 percent in 1989. The average income for the highest decile, which was 16 times greater than the lowest decile in 1984, became 20 times greater in 1989

Excessive and persistent public sector deficits financed through currency issue and decapitalization of the main state enterprises led to a deterioration in income distribution. This happened because of the prolonged inflationary process, the lack of basic needs, and the decline in real salaries. Moreover, the government's decision to concentrate financing on public works was costly to social services.

All of this helped to intensify and increase levels of poverty. As Figure 4.2 illustrates, the percentage of poor families (living below the so-called poverty line) rose from 47 percent in 1984 to 57 percent in 1989.

Survey data show an even greater rise in the number of indigent households; that is, households whose incomes are so low that—even if entirely spent on food—they could not provide adequate family nutrition. This proportion rose from 22.7 percent to 32.5 percent.

Poverty and indigence are more widespread in rural areas than in urban areas. This suggests that the rural population should be given priority in state assistance programs (Santana and Rathe, 1992).

Poverty may have increased even further between 1990 and 1991 since real per capita GDP declined by about 10 percent during this period. The recovery that began in 1991 has not been strong enough to offset the decline. This means that almost two-thirds of the Dominican population now live in poverty.

The current situation must be confronted with strong and decisive measures that will enable the country to reassign public spending, renew interest in social issues, and create a more efficient and effective social services delivery system.

Public Social Spending

Social policy in the Dominican Republic is characterized by a poor social services delivery system that results from limited fiscal allocations to the sector.

Figure 4.2. Household Income by Decile Groups, 1984 and 1989
(1990 RD$)

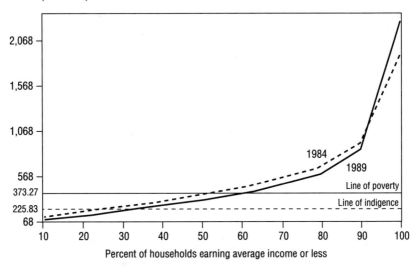

Percent of households earning average income or less

Source: ECOCARIBE, based on 1984 and 1989 Household Income and Expenditure Surveys.

The country's overall social spending—which historically has been below 20 percent of GDP—is relatively low compared to that of other countries. Figure 4.3 shows that social spending during the 1980s reached 20 percent of GDP only in 1988.

Following the 1990-91 economic relapse caused by the restrictive adjustment policies, spending rose again in 1992. It reached 19.3 percent of GDP, thanks to several fiscal measures that allowed for tax increases. However, its absolute value in real terms is still lower than the levels achieved in 1987 and 1988 and is even lower in per capita terms.

These levels are significantly lower than Latin American averages, a fact that becomes more striking when one considers that public spending in the region is generally lower than the worldwide average. For example, as Santana and Rathe (1992) point out, average public spending worldwide in 1986 was 40.4 percent of GDP. (The rate was slightly higher for developed countries.) However, average public spending in Latin America in 1984 amounted to 29.37 percent, the proportion being even lower in the Dominican Republic.

The current global trend is to reduce public spending as a proportion of a country's total spending. However, it is widely agreed that reducing public spending to below minimally acceptable levels is detrimental to the goals of economic development and greater social equality.

Furthermore, limited resources prevent the state from improving its man-

Figure 4.3. Public Expenditure
(Percentage of GDP)

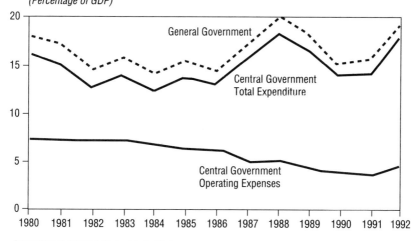

Source: National Statistical Office and Central Bank.

agement capabilities. This, in turn, hampers the ability of state agencies to deliver services and manage programs and projects effectively, to implement policies and control resource allocation adequately, and to enforce laws and impart justice.

Inadequate public spending could also dampen state efforts to create the infrastructure needed for economic development. What is most important is to implement a social policy aimed at eliminating or alleviating poverty, raising the living standards of the population, and training human capital. Such policy, while allowing Latin American countries to successfully participate in the world economy, would require that a significant portion of GDP be assigned to education, health, and social welfare services.

It is clear that if social reforms are to have a positive impact, the state must allocate a reasonable proportion of GDP to social public spending, with a significant portion of the budget allocated to finance benefits and special programs for the poor. Otherwise, social spending will not play an important role in the welfare of indigent or poor households.

Structure of Public Spending

An efficient social policy requires a public budget structured to support social development, whereby a significant portion of allocations target social sectors. It also requires that priority be given to social services that are most beneficial to society's poorest segments.

An effective social policy also requires an efficient government bureau-cracy that can identify the truly vulnerable and their needs, design effective pro-grams, target adequate resources to meet desired goals, and ensure that programs fulfill their stated objectives.

Fiscal spending and social sector allocations have traditionally been low in the Dominican Republic. Following the fiscal adjustment restraints of the mid-1980s, government spending rose once again. New allocation priorities, however, all but abolished social services delivery. Today, driven by inertia, the system continues to operate precariously.

Despite the high proportion of poor and indigent households, the state has not faced up to its responsibility. Furthermore, since the mid-1980s, the govern-ment has primarily funded the public works sector. Social issues have clearly been a lesser priority.

Implementing this policy has made it necessary to generate enormous fiscal savings to finance investments. This was done, as seen in Figure 4.3, by reducing public operational spending. Services whose main costs consisted of recurrent expenses (such as health and education) were totally ignored.

Government capital outlays increased from 25 percent in 1985 to 63 percent in 1989. Today, these outlays represent almost two-thirds of the entire budget and have represented more than half of the budget in the last six years. This is an unusual situation that occurs in very few countries.

Evolution of Social Spending

Although social spending has deteriorated considerably in recent years, not all programs have been equally affected. Table 4.1 shows the structure of social spending based on two types of expenditures: service-intensive and construc-tion-intensive. As can be seen, the former shows a steeper decline, falling from more than 90 percent of total social spending in the first half the 1980s, to 66 percent in recent years.

Table 4.2 shows an overview of social spending in different regions of the world and the proportion of GDP that governments generally allocate to social services. In order to compare the data of countries whose programs are run by the central government with the data of countries whose programs are carried out by state or local governments, data for both types of governments were included.

Latin America allocates an average of 13.2 percent of GDP to social spend-ing. For countries where data on overall government spending exist, the Dominican Republic shows the lowest level of social spending.

What is most striking about the Dominican Republic is not its low level of social spending, but the programs it targets. An unusually high proportion of spending is concentrated on programs that have the least impact on the country's

Table 4.1. Structure of Central Government Social Spending, Selected Years
(percentage of total social spending)

Spending category	1980	1985	1989	1990	1991
Service-intensive expenditures	**89.00**	**92.94**	**60.00**	**67.01**	**66.13**
Education	32.69	32.60	18.43	20.24	20.86
Sports	1.83	3.92	2.19	2.15	1.97
Health	24.38	23.20	21.69	28.06	26.71
Social welfare	18.28	18.65	9.59	9.08	8.27
Labor	0.38	0.31	0.14	0.16	0.17
Municipal services	9.08	12.00	6.80	6.64	7.27
Community services	2.35	2.26	1.17	0.69	0.87
Construction-intensive expenditures	**11.00**	**7.06**	**40.00**	**32.99**	**33.87**
Housing	4.81	4.68	25.31	17.19	15.24
Sewerage and water supply	6.19	2.38	14.68	15.80	18.63

Source: ONAPRES Budget Performance Report.

poorest segment. These programs are primarily targeted to all social strata of the urban sector. Indeed, public spending on housing, water, and sewerage in the Dominican Republic largely exceeds that of other Latin American countries. The reason is quite simple: spending is allocated to the construction of public works whose ultimate goal is not to increase social welfare, but to enhance the government's image through the financing of major construction projects.

As a result, a large part of the new housing developments have been built on previously constructed sites by demolishing old structures. Also, new units have been assigned to families who already had housing. In fact, much of government spending has been directed to remodeling the country's principal cities rather than to social goals.

Since not all government social spending has the same impact on the living conditions of the poor, the United Nations Development Programme (UNDP) developed the concept of the Spending Index for Human Development Projects. In calculating the index, the following factors are considered: (1) government spending as a proportion of GDP; (2) proportion of government spending allocated to social programs; and (3) proportion of social spending that actually fulfills human goals (UNDP, 1991).

A calculation of the index for the Dominican Republic—based on human priority goals that include only spending on basic education, primary health care, and water supply to poor sectors—yields a surprisingly low index of about 1.3 percent for 1991.[2]

---

[2] In calculating the index, hospital and rural clinic care were considered part of health spending. Figures for spending on water supply were based on the assumption that 25 percent was provided to poor sectors.

Table 4.2. Central Government Social Spending in Countries, Selected Years
(percentage of GDP)

Region or country	Year	Education	Health	Social Sec. and others	Total
World	1987	4.89	5.02	11.38	16.27
Industrialized countries	1987	5.01	5.42	12.09	17.10
Africa	1982	5.11	2.07	3.03	8.14
Asia	1987	3.41	0.85	1.87	5.28
Middle East	1987	5.49	1.78	7.88	13.37
Latin America and Caribbean	1987	4.30	1.83	8.88	13.18
Argentina	1987	4.14	1.46	8.45	12.59
Bahamas	1986	4.28	3.24	2.33	6.61
Barbados	1987	5.82	3.93	8.38	14.20
Chile	1987	4.34	1.88	11.47	5.81
Panama	1987	5.19	5.55	5.46	10.65
Suriname	1986	6.23	1.92	3.86	10.09
Dominican Republic	1987	1.50	1.40	3.38	4.88

Source: Government Finance Statistics Yearbook, 1990, IMF.

The UNDP believes that for a country to enhance its level of human development the index must be at least 5 percent. The Dominican Republic is among the countries that have the lowest index for social spending.

Table 4.3 displays the evolution of social spending in real values for 1980. A decidedly downward trend is particularly noticeable in education and social welfare spending. This decline reached critical levels during 1990-91 when social spending declined in real terms by 30.6 percent and 16.1 percent, respectively. The reduction in real per capita spending is even more striking when one considers the increase in population.

This situation has led to an unprecedented deterioration in the quality of social services. The state has largely neglected the social services that are critical to the poor, such as hospital care, schools, and social welfare.

This situation is alarming because, despite high levels of social awareness and the fact that several social reform projects have been drawn up, no concrete steps have yet been taken to implement these programs.

Health Service

The Public Health System

The institutional structure of health care in the Dominican Republic differs greatly from that in other Latin American countries. The State Secretariat of Public Health and Social Welfare (SESPAS) is the institution responsible for the

Table 4.3. Central Government Social Spending by Category, Selected Years
(millions of RD$ at constant 1980 prices)

Spending category	1980	1985	1989	1990	1991
Total social services	442.6	371.0	574.4	398.4	334.4
Education	144.7	120.9	105.8	80.6	69.8
Sports	8.1	14.5	12.6	8.6	6.6
Health	107.9	86.1	124.6	111.8	89.3
Social Welfare	80.9	69.2	55.1	36.2	27.6
Labor	1.7	1.1	0.8	0.6	0.6
Housing	21.3	17.4	145.4	68.5	51.0
Sewerage and water supply	27.4	8.8	84.3	62.9	62.3
Municipal services	40.2	44.5	39.1	26.5	24.3
Community services	10.4	8.4	6.7	2.8	2.9

Source: ONAPRES Budget Performance Report and other official data.

sector's policy and service delivery. The health care system was designed to provide free universal coverage. Social security institutions, on the other hand, provide coverage only to specific segments of the population.

Other institutions—though not strictly health-related—also help in preserving good health standards. These include the departments of water and sewers and the local agencies in charge of sanitation and city clean up.

The State Secretariat of Public Health (SESPAS)

SESPAS is the country's main institution for public health services, particularly to the poor. The institution controls 79 percent of public sector hospital beds and approximately 52 percent of all hospital beds in the country.

SESPAS has legal jurisdiction over all health-related matters. These include health policy and disease prevention, general and specialized in-patient and out-patient medical treatment, supervision and control of private medical services. SESPAS also has other duties such as recording the country's vital and health statistics, and overseeing health education.

However, the modest allocations to the health sector and the overall operational shortcomings of state agencies have hampered effective fulfillment of these duties. In countries with weak institutional structures, responsibilities prescribed by constitutional mandates and laws are often inconsistent with actual programs.

SESPAS divided the country into eight health regions. Each region has its own office responsible for providing health services to everyone within the assigned area. In practice, however, service management is quite centralized, and regional offices have little decision-making power.

Social Security Institutions

The Dominican Social Security Institute (IDSS) was created in 1948. Coverage is limited to private sector workers with monthly salaries below $160. Social security does not cover private employees with higher salaries, state employees, the informal sector, or families of the insured. One of the system's major problems has been premium evasion by employers and employees who have little confidence in the system's efficiency. Because of limited coverage and under-payments, the IDSS provides coverage for only 360,000 permanent and approximately 76,000 temporary employees. In other words, the IDSS covers only 5.8 percent of the country's total population.

The IDSS is responsible for providing health services to its members. However, it is estimated that one-quarter of the health services provided in IDSS facilities benefits uninsured individuals who access these services outside proper channels.

The Armed Forces and the National Police rely on their own social security program (ISSFAPOL) that provides medical services to subscribers, their immediate families, and to active and retired military personnel. ISSFAPOL also provides medical care to low-income civilians through the so-called Armed Forces' Civic Plan of Action. However, it is estimated that less than 3 percent of the national population benefits from these services.

The Private Sector

Privately sponsored health care is freely allowed in the Dominican Republic. SESPAS is responsible for regulating and supervising the activities of private health facilities. However, because of operational shortcomings, the agency is unable to fulfill its responsibilities. Information on private sector health activities is limited.

The public sector accounts for the highest concentration of hospital beds. Yet most health professionals—including the most qualified—work in the private sector. It is difficult to know exactly how many doctors work in each sector because many of those who work in public hospitals also practice privately. Therefore, private sector participation in health care might actually be greater than what is shown in Table 4.4.

Despite SESPAS' objective of providing coverage to 80 percent of the population (excluding high-income individuals and those covered by social security), some studies have estimated that the institution actually covers only 25 percent of outpatient care and 36 percent of hospital costs (Ramírez, Duarte, and Gómez, 1987).

A 1989 survey on family social spending revealed that the private sector accounted for 57 percent of doctor's appointments. This high percentage results from the state's lack of concern for public health issues and from the

Table 4.4. Major Health Resources by Region and Institutional Sector, 1990[1]

Region	SESPAS	IDSS	ISSFAPOL	Private sector	Total
Hospital beds					
National district	2,167	568	362	2,863	5,960
Other southeast	1,049	503	0	220	1,772
Cibao	2,720	368	0	1,215	4,303
Southeast	978	54	0	165	1,197
Total	6,914	1,493	362	4,463	13,232
Physicians					
National district	1,153	681	274	2,207	4,315
Other southeast	506	168	0	189	863
Cibao	1,003	149	0	687	1,839
Southeast	328	41	0	127	496
Total	2,990	1,039	274	3,210	7,513
Dentists					
National district	52	52	17	746	867
Other southeast	56	19	0	7	82
Cibao	115	21	0	48	184
Southeast	31	7	0	8	46
Total	254	99	17	809	1,179

Sources: SESPAS and the Institute of Population and Development Studies.
Note: [1] Data subject to correction.

emergence of private medical care services for middle- and low-income sectors. There are two categories of health service worth noting. One is a profit-driven subsector that includes medical insurance plans, and the other, a sector made up of several state-subsidized nongovernmental organizations that operate independently.

The Private Business Sector

Most health care facilities in the Dominican Republic are privately run. While several of these offer quality services, others (generally those in outlying urban areas) provide substandard care. These services satisfy the demands of lower-income social groups who refuse to use public hospitals, either because they have problems in accessing the services (repeated visits, long waiting periods, etc.) or because they believe that public services are inferior.

However, quality services are available to some low-income households, thanks to a major national program in which clinics provide health care to employees of different institutions and companies.

In 1989, an estimated one-fourth of the population in Santo Domingo was enrolled in some type of private insurance program. Enrollment was less widespread outside of the capital. Many of the companies subscribing to these plans also legally provide IDSS coverage to lower-salaried employees. Consequently, double coverage is quite common. Although this guarantees better coverage for the employee, it implies an extra cost for the company that decreases its economic competitiveness.

Private Nonprofit Institutions

Another category of nonprofit health providers established through civic initiatives includes welfare foundations. These foundations, which receive state subsidies and foreign assistance, charge modest fees for their services.

These institutions have established highly sophisticated hospitals and medical care centers and have made highly specialized services—those either not offered by state hospitals or too costly to be offered by private facilities—available to lower-income groups.

The institutions generally specialize in the treatment of specific diseases and rely on some state assistance, which, however, is not based on particular allocation criteria or clearly defined policies.

The State of Public Health

There is a great need for basic health care reform in the Dominican Republic. The authors of a 1992 World Bank working paper have commented on the inability of hospitals to provide effective patient care because of severe shortages in supplies and equipment. For the most part, hospitals are overstaffed (particularly with doctors), have poor remuneration policies, and lack quality controls or incentives (Lewis, Sulvetta, and Lafogia, 1992, pg. 1).

The government has opted for widespread—but poor-quality—health coverage. Although the long-term results have been unsatisfactory, they have not been totally without impact. General health indicators have improved somewhat over previous years, though overall standards are still considerably lower than those in Latin America. The mortality profile for broad social groups clearly reflects the effects of poverty, inadequate nutrition, overcrowding, and poor environmental health.

Improvements in indicators such as life expectancy at birth, infant mortality, and maternal mortality are clearly a function of a long-term process and are affected by factors not necessarily related to public health care. These factors include urbanization, the development of transportation and communication infrastructures, and higher literacy rates. Table 4.5 presents an overview of the country's current health indicators.

Table 4.5. Health Indicators, Selected Years

Infant mortality (1991)	44.5 per thousand[1]
Urban areas	37.2 per thousand[1]
Rural areas	54.6 per thousand[1]
Mortality among children under 5 (1991)	62.6 per thousand[1]
Urban areas	46.9 per thousand[1]
Rural areas	84.2 per thousand[1]
Maternal mortality (1990)	1 per thousand births
Life expectancy at birth (1990-95)	67 years old
Men	65 years old
Women	69 years old
Principal reasons for consultations, other than pregnancy (1990)	
Acute respiratory diseases	16.9 percent
Acute diarrheal diseases	14.8 percent
Malnutrition and anemia	8.7 percent
Intestinal parasitism	8.4 percent
Diarrheal episodes in children under 5 (1987)	7 per year
Households with access to clean drinking water (1991)	66.6 percent
In the home	20.4 percent
Outside the home	46.2 percent

Source: Data from SESPAS and the Demographic and Health Survey (ENDESA), ONAPLAN-IEPD, 1991.
Note: [1] Rates per thousand live births.

The initiatives undertaken in the last decade to overcome problems in the health sector placed a special emphasis on preventive medicine. Programs included infant immunization against such diseases as polio, mumps, diphtheria, tetanus, whooping cough, and tuberculosis.

While these programs had a strong impact in the mid-1980s, their coverage and effectiveness have somewhat declined. According to the 1991 Health Demographic Survey (ENDESA), almost all children between the ages of 12 months and 24 months have received some type of immunization, but only 36.7 percent have been completely immunized against tuberculosis, mumps, diphtheria, tetanus, whooping cough, and polio.

Distribution of Public Health Spending

Although health services provided by SESPAS are free, patients are charged for lab tests and other diagnostic procedures provided by private health facilities.

Table 4.6. Family Health Spending by Income Group, 1984

Income group	Health expen. ($RD millions)	Percent of total	Per capita spending	Per capita income	Spending as % of income
Low[1]	49.7	14.4	20.66	237.62	8.7
Low middle[2]	97.7	28.2	39.97	801.55	5.0
High middle[3]	135.3	39.1	86.24	2,168.36	4.0
High[4]	63.4	18.3	197.63	7,423.68	2.7
Total	346.1	100.0	51.34	1,115.03	4.6

Source: ENIGF, 1984.
Notes: [1] Includes the poorest 40 percent of all households.
   [2] Includes households in the category between the poorest 40 percent and the richest 25 percent of all families.
   [3] Includes households in the category between the poorest 75 percent and the richest 5 percent of all families.
   [4] Includes the richest 5 percent of all households.

Patients are also responsible for paying for prescription medicines and, occasionally, for hospital disposable materials such as syringes. While the latter is not a hard and fast rule, it is sometimes a necessity because of hospital shortages.

Results of a 1984 national survey on family income and expenditures (ENIGF) revealed that household spending on health amounted to RD$346.1 billion (see Table 4.6). Public spending on health for the same year amounted to RD$146.5 million. This means that 70 percent of total health spending was for private services and 30 percent for public services. The ENIGF survey recorded only family spending. Since companies pay a significant part of medical insurance programs, private sector contributions may even be higher. Table 4.6 shows that private sector health spending increases proportionally with social level. The per capita spending of the wealthiest 5 percent of the population is 10 times higher than that of the poorest group. However, health spending represents a much heavier burden for the poorest group (8.7 percent of income) than for high-income groups (2.7 percent of income).

The poor spend less on health, in absolute terms, than the wealthy, despite living in substandard conditions of sanitation and nutrition. Partially attributable to government health assistance initiatives, this situation also reflects the inability of lower-income groups to pay for goods and services that would ensure adequate health standards. In general, the poorest segment of the population receives care in government clinics and can hardly pay for prescription drugs. The latter account for 57 percent of lower-income spending on health and 40 percent of higher-income spending.

The survey revealed that 19 percent of private doctor visits in 1984 were made by the poorest 40 percent of households, and 30 percent, by the lower middle-income group. In other words, 56 percent of the beneficiaries of private medical services belonged to the poorest 75 percent of the population.

A 1991 survey of SESPAS hospital patients evaluated the distribution of public spending on health. The survey was conducted by the authors of this chapter within the context of a previous study as part of the Centers for Research in Applied Economics Project. Results of the study were published in Santana and Rathe (1992).

Although families of different income levels receive, in one form or another, part of public health spending benefits, the proportion is greater among the poorer households. For example, households with the lowest 43.5 percent of incomes received 59.6 percent of public benefits. The highest-income level received only 13.3 percent. These results confirm that, had it not been for state action, these households would have had minimal access to health services. This, in turn, confirms that government health spending is an efficient mechanism for redistribution of national income.

High-income households make less use of public services and, therefore, receive fewer public health benefits. Although high-income households account for 61 percent of the national income, 23.5 percent of the wealthiest families receive only 18.8 percent of benefits.

The previously cited study pointed out that the Lorenz curves, which reflect distribution in national income and public health benefits, show that the public health benefit curve lies above the diagonal. This not only means that benefits are better distributed than national income, but that the poor benefit more in absolute terms. It can be concluded, therefore, that public spending on health is an adequate mechanism for improving income distribution and reducing poverty.

The study further concludes that relatively high-income sectors also receive government benefits. If the government's aim in providing health services is to benefit only the poor, it would be counterproductive to subsidize higher-income groups. This perhaps suggests the feasibility of seeking a mechanism whereby higher-income groups would pay for at least the cost of services they receive.

Education Service

Organizational Structure of the Education System

The education system in the Dominican Republic is governed by Law 2909 enacted in 1951. The law provides for free public elementary and secondary education. The law also establishes education levels and regulates the evaluation of degrees, diplomas, and textbooks. In addition to the Basic Education Law, a large number of other legal texts exist (agreements, decrees, ordinances and resolutions), resulting in a highly diffuse and complex legal framework. The difficulty of managing such a large and complex volume of legal texts has been the subject of several analyses and studies.

The State Secretariat of Education, Fine Arts, and Culture (SEEBAC) is responsible for all educational activities up to the secondary level. SEEBAC was established as a national agency with overall responsibilities over education, including policy formulation, regulation, supervision, and direct delivery of services. The secretariat is located in the capital of the republic. For practical reasons, it has divided the country into regional offices and school districts.

Several studies have underlined the lack of administrative criteria governing the system's operations. This deficiency has resulted in incoherent and disjointed decision making; excessive centralization of authority within the secretariat; and inadequate administrative career paths and remuneration and inconsistency between legally prescribed and actual status of structures. These problems also reflect on SEEBAC's low technical competence since the agency lacks procedures for hiring and evaluating personnel. Low salaries also make it difficult to hire or keep qualified personnel.

In late 1992, after numerous studies and discussions, and after much pressure from various civic and international organizations, the government developed the Ten-Year Education Plan in an effort to improve the sector.

Structure of Public Education

SEEBAC controls elementary (including pre-school), secondary, and special education, as well as several adult education programs. Universities, however, operate independently of the secretariat.

Early Education

The provisions of the Basic Education Law do not address early education, which is administered by government resolutions. SEEBAC has a Department of Pre-School Education. However, the government provides minimal services at this level. In 1990, the number of children between the ages of 3 and 6 was estimated to be about 766,000. However, fewer than 20,000 were enrolled in pre-school programs. Private pre-school services have traditionally been available to higher-income groups but not to most of the country's households.

Elementary Education

Elementary education is compulsory and free for children between the ages of 7 and 14. Although the law mandates compulsory education until the sixth grade, a 1986 resolution of the National Council on Education extended compulsory attendance until the eighth grade. However, the resolution has not been carried out in practice because the state does not have the means to enforce compulsory education nor the resources to make it universally available.

Table 4.7 displays population and public enrollment data by age for the 1989-90 school year. It can be observed that public elementary school coverage

Table 4.7. Public Elementary School Enrollment in the Dominican Republic, 1989-90 School Year

Age	Child population (thousands)	Public enrollment (thousands)	Percentage of enrollment
7	179.7	101.9	56.7
8	175.9	103.9	59.0
9	172.0	103.1	59.9
10	168.1	108.2	64.4
11	164.0	103.5	63.1
12	160.8	107.6	66.9
13	158.7	99.2	62.5
14	157.4	77.9	49.5
Total	1,336.6	805.3	60.2

Source: National Office of Statistics, 1992.

for children between the ages of 7 and 14 is only 60.2 percent. However, if children under the age of 7 and, in particular, those over the age of 14 are included, coverage rises to 71 percent.

Secondary Education

SEEBAC's General Office of Secondary Education is responsible for managing the four years of secondary education. Enrollment at this level is more prominent in urban areas, where 93 percent of all private and public schools operate. The level includes high schools and technical-professional training schools. The latter training is offered by some schools to senior high school students. Only 3.5 percent of all high school students follow this course of study.

Secondary education in the Dominican Republic is strictly traditional in that it offers a four-year curriculum that prepares students for university studies but does not offer them the training they need to enter the job market. Therefore, too many high school graduates choose to enroll in universities, leading to overcrowded conditions and inferior quality of these institutions.

The Private Sector

The education system in the Dominican Republic is quite liberal. SEEBAC's control and supervision of private education has traditionally been lax. This attitude was justifiable when private education represented a small portion of formal education and served the needs of higher-income groups. For example, in 1970 private schools accounted for only 10 percent of elementary and 17 percent of secondary enrollments and for only a small percentage of higher education enrollment. However, private education has grown considerably over the past two decades (see Figures 4.4 and 4.5), a direct result of the government's neglect of education and the deterioration in the quality of public schools.

Today private schools account for 56 percent of pre-school, 22 percent of elementary (almost 50 percent in urban areas), and 31 percent of high school enrollments. A large number of poor-quality private schools operate outside the formal education system in poor urban areas.

Higher Education

Universities operate as autonomous entities outside SEEBAC's supervision and control. The 1970s saw a proliferation of private institutes of higher learning that offered inferior education and conferred unqualified degrees. In response to this situation, a law was passed in 1983 creating the National Council for Higher Education (CONES). This entity advises the government on how to regulate the sector.

The Dominican Republic has one state university that was founded by the Spanish in the 16th century and is the oldest university in the Americas. This institution receives almost all of its funding (more than 80 percent) from the government. Tuition fees are quite low and are viewed more as token contributions by the student body.

The state university accounts for 25 percent of total enrollment in higher education, which in 1989 amounted to 122,335 students. The country also has 23 private universities and 5 institutes of higher learning. Four universities are religiously affiliated (2 Catholic, 1 Adventist, and 1 Evangelical) and account for 9 percent of enrollment. The remaining facilities include both nonprofit institutions supported by trusts and foundations and by other facilities that operate as private businesses.

Little factual information is available for evaluating the quality of education provided by the different types of universities. Degrees granted by the state university have traditionally received greater acceptance. However, the university experienced a significant academic decline during the 1970s that still persists. Despite a lack of information on private universities, the low level of recognition and instabilities affecting some institutions leads one to conclude that the instruction they provide is far from adequate. Degrees granted by Catholic universities and by universities sponsored by nonprofit organizations are the most prestigious.

Status of Education Services

Except for a setback in the 1980s, coverage has increased over the long term for practically every level of education in the Dominican Republic. However, quality of education has declined.

Figure 4.4. Trend of Middle School Registration
(Thousands of students)

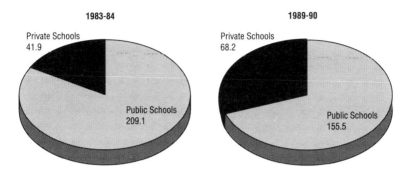

Source: ECOCARIBE, based on National Statistical Office's report, *Education in the Dominican Republic* (1970-92).

Figure 4.5. Trend of Elementary School Registration
(Thousands of students)

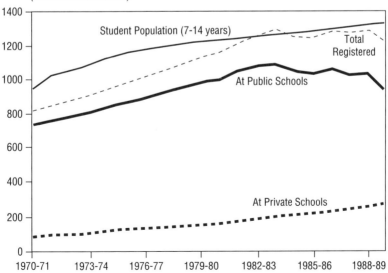

Source: ECOCARIBE, based on National Statistical Office's report, *Education in the Dominican Republic (1970-92).*

Statistical Profile

The country's illiteracy rate has decreased dramatically over the years, falling from 60 percent in 1950 to 25 percent in 1981. In 1991, ENDESA statistics showed that 17.5 percent of the population over 6 years of age had no formal education. This percentage is almost double in rural areas. It should be pointed out that the illiteracy rate might be higher than the figures indicate. This is because census data classify as literate those individuals who claim to know how to read and write. It is clear, however, that many who so claimed are unable to assess their degree of literacy.

The average number of years of schooling for the population over 6 years of age is 4.7 for men and 5.4 for women. The average number of years of schooling rises to 6.8 in urban areas but drops to 2.8 in rural areas, a figure comparable to that of many of the world's poorest countries.

Education coverage has also improved considerably in recent decades. As Figure 4.5 shows, elementary education has been available for many years to 100 percent of the school-age population. At times, coverage has even exceeded 100 percent. The obvious explanation for this is that total enrollment includes students who, because of missed classes, have fallen behind in grade levels. According to ENDESA, 16 percent of the children between the ages of 6 and 15 do not attend school.

Figure 4.5 also shows a recent decline, in absolute terms, of elementary public school enrollment that implies a drop in total enrollment. Apparently, this is the result of the marked deterioration in the living standards of many households in recent years. Fortunately, recent SEEBAC statistics indicate that this trend has begun to reverse itself. In the 1992-93 school year, 1.5 million children were enrolled in public pre-schools and elementary schools.

High school education, which is almost exclusively concentrated in urban areas, has also declined since 1983-84, as Figure 4.4 shows. Public sector enrollment declined from 209,100 students to 155,500 students in 1989-90. Despite an increase in population and in the number of private schools, total student enrollment still dropped by 11 percent.

Quality in Education

The education system in the Dominican Republic has significant shortcomings that detract from the quality of their services. The outcome has been high student dropout and failure rates and students falling behind in grade levels. A major problem is low coverage in pre-school education. Children who start elementary school without having attended pre-school find themselves at a real disadvantage. They are more likely to fail or drop out of the system without having developed basic learning skills.

Table 4.8. National Exam Results and Grades Given in Eighth Grade Courses, 1992
(percent)

Subject	National Exams		Grades Given in Class	
	Pass	Fail	Pass	Fail
Spanish	36	64	81	19
Mathematics	38	62	80	20
Social sciences	59	41	70	30
Natural sciences	50	50	88	12

Source: SEEBAC, 1992.

In terms of age, 55.3 percent of first graders and 70.1 percent of second graders exceeded the age appropriate for their grade level in the 1986-87 school year. The failure rate in elementary schools hovers around 17 percent and reaches 30 percent for first grade. The dropout rate is also high, reaching 10 percent in 1987-88. It is estimated that only 19 percent of students who begin their education in public schools finish on schedule. This figure is 40 percent for the secondary level.

Several partial studies have been carried out on the general quality of education. Almost all studies conclude that the competence of graduates at all levels is lower than required or planned (Díaz Santana, *et al.*, 1990). As Díaz Santana *et al.* (1990) point out, an evaluation carried out by SEEBAC in 1984 revealed that most students who completed the first cycle of elementary education (grades 1 through 4) received, on the average, grades of 40 or less.

In 1992, SEEBAC instituted compulsory national tests at the eighth grade level as a requirement to enter high school. The results of these tests confirmed the results of the studies carried out, as can be seen in Table 4.8.

The table displays the students' overall poor academic results, particularly in two main areas: Spanish and mathematics. However, a high percentage of students were promoted because of the cumulative average of the grades they received during the school year.

Despite the fact that almost 90 percent of elementary school teachers have degrees, studies have shown that these degrees do not necessarily guarantee high academic quality because of basic shortcomings in teacher training programs (Díaz Santana, 1988). Moreover, almost one-half of elementary school teachers work two shifts daily, which inevitably affects the quality of their teaching.

Teacher salaries are among the lowest in the country. SEEBAC (1992) points out that, in 1990, elementary school teachers earned only one-seventh of what they earned in 1970. The recent minimum salary adjustment for industrial workers has made industrial salaries higher than those of teachers who work only one shift, which means that in many cases unskilled laborers receive higher salaries.

Table 4.9. Public Education Spending by Program, Selected Years
(millions of 1980 Dominican pesos)

Program	1980	1985	1989	1990	1991
Administrative costs	8.7	6.0	3.6	6.9	4.2
Pre-school education	1	0.7	0.5	0.4	0.4
Elementary education	44.6	46.0	33.6	26.1	16.7
Secondary education	18.8	15.6	9.9	6.9	4.3
Higher education	29.6	19.6	15.9	11.9	10.4
Technical education	3.5	5.0	5.0	4.8	4.5
Adult education	4.0	4.7	3.3	2.3	1.4
Student physical education	1.7	0.9	1.0	0.9	0.7
Teacher training	2.0	1.0	1.1	0.5	0.3
Technical-educational support	0.4	2.3	1.9	2.1	1.3
Culture and fine arts	3.6	2.3	1.8	1.2	1.5
Others[2]	27.8	16.9	28.3	16.5	23.9
Total	144.7	120.9	105.8	80.6	69.8

Source: ONAPRES Budget Performance Report.
Notes: [1] Included in elementary education.
[2] Includes construction expenditures by the Office of the President of the Republic.

Financing of Education

According to the 1984 national survey on family income and expenditures (ENIGF), education in the Dominican Republic has been financed primarily by the private sector. Households spent RD$236 million on education, while the government spent RD$212 million.

During the first half of the 1980s, the government allocated just over 2 percent of GDP to education. This rate, while already low, has continued to decline even further. In early 1990 it fluctuated between 1 percent and 1.2 percent of GDP. A reversal of this trend began in 1992, when spending reached 1.3 percent of GDP.

Table 4.9 shows the evolution of spending on education by program for the period 1980-91. The data show a significant drop in education spending, particularly at the elementary and secondary levels. Indeed, total spending for the period decreased by 51.8 percent, but spending on elementary education, which amounted to 0.22 percent of GDP, fell to one-third of its earlier level. Spending on secondary education dropped by 77 percent, less than one-quarter below its previous level. Spending on higher education fell by 65 percent.

State spending per student for 1991 was 232 pesos at the elementary level, and 397 pesos at the secondary level. In terms of private spending on education, middle-class households spent about RD$6,000 per student at the elementary level and RD$8,000 at the secondary level. These figures do not include other education-related expenses. This means that a household spends in two weeks what the state spends over the entire year for the education of one child.

Figure 4.6. School Attendance in 1984
(percentage)

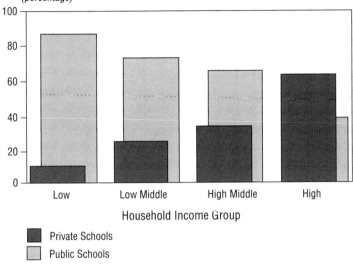

Source: ECOCARIBE, based on the 1984 Household Income and Expenditure Survey.

Beneficiaries of Public Spending on Education

There is a definite correlation between income level and private school enrollment. This is illustrated in Figure 4.6, which shows that a high percentage of
children who belong to low- and middle-income families attend private schools.
Indeed, in 1984 (survey year on which the figure is based), 47 percent of the
population was living at a critical level of poverty. This proportion includes all
low-income and a portion of lower middle-income families. Given the country's
relatively low level of development, the upper-income tier—which includes 5
percent of the highest-income families—comprises the truly wealthy and also
the so-called urban middle class. Therefore, many of the families at the upper
middle-income level can be considered to be poor or lower middle-class.

A study on spending by Ceara and Croes (1992) provides figures on public
and private school attendance in 1989 by family income level (see Table 4.10).
However, because income levels are grouped differently, comparison with the
1984 data is not possible.

As can be seen in the table, the distribution in school attendance among
children of different income families is more widespread than the income distribution of the families. In other words, although income is concentrated at the
higher level, the poor have access to education thanks, mainly, to government

Table 4.10. Distribution of Students by Income Group and Type of School, 1989
(percent)

Income groups	Income[1]	Total attendance	Public school attendance	Private school attendance
Poorest 50 percent	13.2	53.5	64.9	35.3
Middle 40 percent	42.5	37.8	32.8	45.9
Wealthiest 10 percent	44.2	8.7	2.3	18.8

Source: Ceara and Croes (1992).
Note: [1] Group's income as percentage of national total.

efforts. This feature is even more pronounced when one looks at public school attendance. However, it is regrettable that only 35 percent of private enrollment comes from the poorest 50 percent of households.

In any event, it is clear that public spending on education constitutes an adequate distribution mechanism, particularly in elementary education. It is also necessary to keep in mind that public spending on education brings long-term social and economic improvements as well as increases in overall economic productivity.

The Social Welfare System

Structure of the System

The Dominican Republic has no structured welfare system in place, despite the fact that the country's constitution assigns the state a primary role in social welfare and that the country has 4.5 million poor, 2.5 million of whom live in abject poverty. The country's formal social security system barely provides partial coverage for less than 10 percent of the population, leaving most of the country's population unprotected against old age, disability, indigence, disease, and other contingencies.

In addition to a social security program, the country has implemented wide-ranging but still tenuous independent social assistance initiatives. These have relied on discretionary government allocations and have been subjected to the biases of the officials responsible for managing those funds. In any event, resources allocated to the sector have been minimal, amounting in 1991 to only 0.1 percent of GDP. While several of the existing social welfare programs had a significant impact in their early days, they have now lost their importance due to changes in government priorities. Funds currently available to the programs are meager. However, given the necessary resources, their existing operating structure could conduct social activities with a certain degree of effectiveness.

Social Assistance of SESPAS

The role of SESPAS is to tend to the social welfare of the population. The agency's Subsecretariat of Social Assistance is responsible for doling out public social assistance. The law defines social assistance as (1) fixed aid or family subsidy; (2) occasional financial aid for emergency and pressing needs; (3) organized distribution of staple supplies (dietary supplements and child nutrition); and (4) all assistance involving physical relief or improvements in the status of the needy.

The Subsecretariat operates through specialized departments established to assist specific segments of the community. These departments include Child Protective Services, whose purpose is to care for abandoned children; Day Care Nurseries for poor children; School Homes for children with adjustment problems; Nonagenarian and Centenarian Offices, which grant pensions to elderly indigents; Geriatric Centers, which provide care to elderly indigents; the Social Welfare Office, which furnishes fixed welfare aid to people unable to work; and the Supplementary Food Office, which helps reduce infant malnutrition in children under the age of two through daily rations of milk. While it is clear that a structure to carry out social welfare programs is in place, the lack of resources has now rendered the entire welfare apparatus inoperable.

In 1990, the subsecretariat provided partial assistance to 919 residents in 13 retirement homes, 700 beneficiaries in six day care centers, and 900 beneficiaries in five school homes. The subsecretariat had previously administered a pension program for octogenarians and nonagenarians. However, this program has deteriorated because of lack of resources. It consists today of monthly stipends of less than RD$100 paid to a group of elderly that in 1990 numbered 4,146.

Office of the President of the Republic

The Office of the President is also involved in several social assistance initiatives. Two worth mentioning are the National Council for Children (CONANI) and the food assistance program. In addition to these programs and the pension funds, the presidency's social assistance program involves gifts the president bestows personally during his frequent visits to impoverished urban sectors and rural areas. This practice, part of his continuous presidential campaign, dates back to the middle of this century.

The National Council for Children

The purpose of the CONANI, which was created in 1978, is to promote child welfare through the study, coordination, implementation, and support of plans, initiatives, and programs designed to benefit children. This council has been active in the areas of health, nutrition, informal pre-school and elementary education, psychology, and social work. Despite the program's early impact, it has been beleaguered in later years by the same budgetary problems that affect the sector as a whole.

The country has 37 centers currently in operation that provide direct assistance to pre-school and elementary education, supplementary nutrition, and health care for 6,500 children. The council's low budget is almost totally depleted by operating costs, which makes it difficult to implement truly efficient initiatives that would benefit thousands of poor and indigent street children in the country's main cities. In real value terms, CONANI outlays declined by 73 percent between 1981 and 1991.

Food Kitchens

One of the country's most effective social service programs is the Food Kitchen Program, which the government established in 1971. Currently there are 83 food kitchens in the country. These centers are generally located in impoverished urban neighborhoods, close to work sites such as sugar factories or industrial zones, or in the poorest rural villages. The kitchens also provide food to prisons, several orphanages, and nursing homes. With adequate resources and management, this program could effectively benefit the poor. The location of the kitchens in disadvantaged areas and the long waiting periods have kept high-income sectors from availing themselves of the program. Also, low food prices have led people to question the quality of the service.

The main problem of the Food Kitchen Program, which was established as a low-cost food delivery service, is that food prices were not adjusted for inflation. In 1990, the price of a meal was 35 cents in Dominican pesos. Today the price is one peso, even though in 1992 the government paid more than 10 pesos for each meal.[3] With the prices they charge for food decreasing rapidly over time, it has been difficult to raise the capital needed to expand the program and lessen its dependency on public funds. Therefore, the program's impact is negligible. The number of rations served in 1992 was 9 million. Providing just one meal a day to the 2.5 million indigents living in the Dominican Republic would mean serving more than 900 million rations a year. This illustrates the program's limited reach.

Distributive Effect of Spending on Social Assistance

In 1980, not counting the social security system, the government allocated about RD$41.3 million (0.6 percent of GDP) to social assistance programs. This figure

---

[3] This amount includes kitchen overhead costs.

dropped, in 1980 real value terms, to RD$9.0 million in 1991 (0.1 percent of GDP). Since assistance programs for the unemployed, the disabled, the elderly, and the indigent were no longer in operation, although they still appeared as part of social assistance budget, a large portion of social outlays were used to defray bureaucratic costs.

Even in the absence of reliable data, it can be safely argued that public social spending is targeted to low-income groups. It can also be argued that social welfare activities have a favorable impact on national income distribution, but a limited impact on the welfare of poor families.

Toward an Agenda for Social Reform

A stable legal, institutional, and macroeconomic framework that allows and encourages productive investments will improve living standards through higher employment, productivity, and salary levels. Progress has been made in these areas as the country's economy has stabilized and begun to grow again.

The country is undergoing in-depth reform designed to overhaul obsolete structures and bring them in line with the changing national economy. A goal of the reforms is to increase economic openness, so that the country can success- fully participate in the changing world economy. The process has helped raise the level of national expectations concerning possibilities for country's future development.

However, it is generally agreed that these reforms will not be totally effec- tive unless they are accompanied by others that can establish an adequate social services delivery system, a truly democratic state, and stronger institutions.

The social policy experience of the Dominican Republic had little success. Public concern for funding social sector activities has been minimal. While the country's social indicators have improved somewhat over the long term, they are still quite low as compared to other Latin American countries (see Table 4.11).

Much of the Dominican population are unable to solve their own problems without help from the state. The state has a responsibility to these citizens that it must honor. It can do so by implementing a series of programs that encourage individual development. Priority should be given to policies that help the poor develop the capabilities and attitudes they need to overcome poverty through their own efforts. This means working to surmount obstacles that have impeded their access to equal opportunities since birth.

One of the first steps that should be taken to reform social services delivery is to refocus the system and the state's role within it. The new focus should emphasize the state's main responsibility as providing efficient social services. It should also stress the importance of placing a high priority on services that are most beneficial to the poor.

The positive effects of investments in human capital are apparent only in the long term. Governments are generally cost-conscious. Returns should be evalu-

Table 4.11. Social Indicators in the Dominican Republic and Latin America, 1991

	Dominican Republic	Latin America
Education		
Elementary school registration (percent of age group)	84	102
Secondary school registration (percent of age group)	36	45
Student/elementary teacher ratio	47	28
Illiteracy rate (percent of population)	17.5	15.3
Health and welfare		
Infant mortality (per thousand live births)	44.3	47.3
Life expectancy at birth (years)	66.0	67.0
Availability of drinking water (percent of households)	66.6	78.5
Daily per capita calorie consumption	2,359	2,737

Source: ONE, 1992; IEPD, 1992; ONAPLAN-IEPD-CELADE, 1991.

ated over the entire maturation period of the investment, which makes it difficult to measure the results of the human capital investment during the finite term of individual administrations. Thus creating mechanisms that enable social reforms to endure is necessary.

During the 1991 crisis of the services delivery system, the public adopted a highly activist attitude and pressured the government, through different organizations, to focus on the issue. The government responded by assigning working groups to analyze the problem and prepare detailed reports on the status of the education and health sectors. A series of economic and institutional reforms was then proposed to improve operations in the two sectors. Decisions on many of these reforms are still pending.

A similar situation occurred in social welfare. From the outset of the economic adjustment program, accompanying social welfare measures that would compensate the groups most seriously affected by the crisis were recommended. Creation of a social welfare fund endowed with sizeable resources contributed by the government and supplemented by foreign aid was also advised.

Delays and indecision in the social sectors are caused by the greater resource allocations needed before any potential solution can be applied. However, the government seems unwilling to allocate more resources to the sector. Most countries have difficulty implementing reforms that involve restructuring fiscal budgets because of the commitments and political and economic pressures under which governments operate. But when there is a lack of will, obstacles tend to be overstated.

Despite these problems, some minor improvements have been achieved. Attention to health and education—though still lagging behind international standards—was considerably greater in 1992 than in previous years and could increase even further in the next year or so.

Means of Financing Social Services

All of society should be committed to objectives that seek a marked increase in social resources for alleviating and reducing poverty, an enhancement in the quality of services provided, and improvements in human resources that underpin economic development. Such objectives require increasing fiscal allocations to the social sector, which must be done within the framework of institutional reforms. Such reforms must rely on the efforts of all society and on the private sector's cost-recovery programs.

Increasing Public Social Spending

There is a close relationship between levels of public social spending and improvements in indicators of social progress and human development. Public spending on the three sectors studied here—education, health, and social welfare—should be augmented. The goal should be to increase spending over a two-to-three year period from 2.8 percent of GDP (in 1992) to 8 percent, as follows: 4 percent for education, 2.5 percent for health, and 1.5 percent for social welfare. This might seem to be an ambitious goal. However, it is reasonable when one considers the experience of other countries in which social spending goals are achieved.

Implementing programs that guarantee allocation of at least 80 percent of social resources to half of the country's poor would raise the beneficiaries' contribution to the national income to about 23 percent, up from the current 17 percent. Other spending (sports and recreation, community services, environmental health, promotion of agriculture, irrigation, transportation, etc.) could supplement these allocations.

Higher government outlays are needed to achieve this objective. This could be accomplished by increasing taxes above the 18 percent assessed in 1992. Another alternative for increasing social spending might be to make budgetary cuts in other areas of public spending, which today accounts for about 20 percent of GDP. This alternative could be implemented within the current tax regime.

The following steps could be taken to raise social spending to 10 percent of GDP. First, social sector outlays could be increased to represent half of the budget, while outlays for infrastructure, urban projects, and subsidy programs to state enterprises (for example, to the State Council on Sugar and the Dominican Electric Company) could be decreased. The latter sectors, while important, are not critical. A special effort should also be made to reduce the country's debt-servicing burden.

Second, 80 percent of social spending could be allocated to the health, education, and social welfare sectors, on the premise that these sectors are the state's most important objectives. This could be accomplished by dramatically reducing housing expenditures. It is important for a country beset by so many critical needs to establish its priorities clearly.

Spending within the three sectors should also be restructured. Currently, only 40 percent of the sectors' allocations satisfy the criteria set by the UNDP for high human priority, requiring thus new emphasis on basic services in education, health, and social welfare.

Education should receive its fair share of spending. Expectations for economic growth are largely based on increased export of primary goods and not necessarily on education. However, current global economic trends suggest an international environment in which knowledge would provide the competitive edge. Thus, if the country aspires to keep up with these trends and have any hope of success, education must be given special attention. The previously suggested goal of allocating 4 percent of GDP to the education sector would mean a three-fold increase in the education budget, a totally feasible objective. Improvements in sector salaries and work conditions would be required in order to support the teaching profession and to attract and retain talented and qualified teachers.

If education spending is to become a truly effective vehicle for social improvement, greater priority must be given to pre-school and elementary education. These levels of education are most beneficial to the poor and also fulfill the mandate for free compulsory elementary and secondary education.

In health, where public spending is excessively low, spending should be raised to 2.5 percent of GDP, thereby doubling the sector's budget. This increase would serve, in part, to raise the level of personnel qualifications and salaries and to improve the availability of hospital equipment and services.

Improving social welfare may prove a slow process since the Dominican Republic is still unable to implement efficient assistance programs that address issues of unemployment, single mothers, and the subsistence of the indigent population. It should be essential to create a permanent social welfare fund of at least 1.5 percent of GDP. The fund would fulfill the following three functions: (1) transfer resources to nongovernmental organizations dedicated to the comprehensive care of the elderly and children; (2) provide family nutrition—education assistance would include nutritional assistance to children but would not include all family members. Any food subsidy program for poor households would need community cooperation. Also included could be a special maternal-child nutrition program administered as part of health programs, similar to those which already exist in Latin America; (3) assistance for community development projects with participatory efforts by interested parties, particularly in rural areas and disadvantaged urban areas. The projects would include tasks such as rehabilitation and road maintenance, housing improvements, reforestation, and environmental health.

Cost Recovery

Adopting cost-recovery measures could help make funds available for public assistance to health, education, and social welfare services. Although public preschool and elementary education should continue to be free as a way to foster universal coverage, tuition fees could be charged at the secondary level for some students. Community participation will help ensure that tuition fees are assessed only on families who can afford them.

A similar approach should be taken for hospital charges. While primary health care should, in principle, remain free, research has shown that many patients are able to pay at least part of the cost. Decentralization and community participation should ease cost-recovery schemes and minimize adverse effects on the needy. As hospital facilities become increasingly able to cover maintenance and supply procurement costs, thanks to cost-recovery programs, the state could gradually reduce allocations for these expenses.

Needed Institutional Reforms

Social reform also means public reform. Reform enables the state's modernization, increases its efficiency, and redefines its interaction with society. Reform also implies transferring responsibilities to community organizations and their representatives while maintaining the state's prerogative to define national priorities, formulate policies, redistribute resources, and establish and enforce the rules under which society operates.

The Dominican Republic cannot implement an efficient social policy program unless major changes are made in the way institutions operate. Resources are currently being drained by the apathy of an excessively large and inefficient bureaucracy. Services do not achieve intended objectives because they are inferior. Contributing to this problem are unqualified or uncommitted personnel who also quite often have too many responsibilities. Thus, current programs are not helpful to the most vulnerable segment of the population, while the government finds itself incapable of formulating better programs.

Institutional changes must be designed to achieve the following objectives: focusing in those programs where it is feasible; deconcentrating duties in central administration; decentralizing responsibilities in order to make management of services more democratic; and, finally, involving the community.

Targeting

In societies in which poverty is not widespread and an efficient bureaucracy and an ample and effective information system exist, targeting is the most efficient means by which any social program will have a positive impact on income distribution. However, this is not the case in most Latin American countries and particularly in the Dominican Republic, a country with widespread poverty, a practically nonexistent information system, and a state apparatus plagued by inefficiency and corruption. Without knowing precisely how many poor live in the country, where they live, and who they are, subsidy allocations should not be left to unqualified individuals who are not always honest and who, moreover, operate without proper control and supervision.

The poorest segment of the population generally lacks information and, in particular, the ability to organize itself for the purpose of exerting political leverage and influencing decision making. Therefore, the poor are at a disadvantage in their struggle for social benefits and public allocations. The Dominican Republic's state-financed housing program, which generally benefits middle- and high-income sectors, illustrates this point.

Targeting is not feasible for some government programs, while for others it is essential. In health and elementary education, targeting is unnecessary because beneficiaries constitute a large segment of the population and the state has a basic obligation to provide these services to its citizens for the good of the country. This implies that allocations based on the principle of free, universal coverage should continue to constitute a major portion of social spending. The private sector, for its part, will always provide coverage to certain groups, but this should be the exception, not the rule.

Targeting is more appropriate in higher education and for technical training. Users of these services are limited in number, and their income group can easily be determined. In this case, serious consideration should be given to channeling the state university's government subsidies to a scholarship program.

Targeting is essential—though not easily achieved—in social welfare programs. Community involvement can help ensure that funds targeted for the poor not be used by higher-income groups.

Even if a new fund allocation system were less than perfect and allowed higher-income groups to benefit from social programs, it would still be preferable to accepting the government's inertia and inactivity in the face of the current monumental human drama.

Decentralization

Today, closer ties are being forged between government officials responsible for delivering social services and the communities receiving them. It is clear that closer community ties and a greater awareness of community needs and aspirations heighten the commitment of authorities to confronting social problems. Closer ties also increase opportunities for the community to participate in decision making in matters affecting their welfare, for streamlining public spending, and for simplifying community problem-solving procedures.

Simplifying and streamlining bureaucracy and introducing a more rational allocation and control of resources would help decentralization in the Dominican Republic. Above all, gradually strengthening local authorities would enhance democratic processes. These organizations lost much of their resources, operational capabilities, and responsibilities within their communities when, several decades ago, almost all of Latin America viewed centralization as the means for achieving a planned economy and universal coverage.

One of the first steps toward decentralizing the social sector is the political restructuring of the municipal system. Separation of national and municipal elections is also vital, allowing community attention to be focused on the selection process and on choosing the best-prepared candidates. The community's greater political power, and the responsibility toward their constituents would encourage more competent individuals to run.

These two steps should significantly strengthen municipal institutions. Gradually increasing allocations of public funds to city councils and enhancing their responsibility in daily decisions on environmental health, maintenance and rehabilitation of roads, traffic signs, overland traffic, infrastructures, supporting services, and other minor community services is also important.

In order to develop municipal experience in tax collection, local authorities should be responsibile for collecting local taxes such as road tolls, vehicle registration taxes, and property taxes. In this way, the municipalities would strengthen their capacity to administer resources and exert financial control. The community will also show greater interest in local activities and will be able to develop mechanisms for monitoring the activities of local authorities.

The central government should train municipal personnel in matters of administration, accounting, statistics, data processing, project evaluation, and other areas linked to the allocation and management of resources. It is also necessary to legislate a series of minimum civil service requirements at the municipal level. These conditions would prevent political abuse in personnel management without restricting the municipality's capacity for self-government.

The trend in social services should be to transfer to municipalities, over a reasonable period of time, all authority regarding direct service delivery and to preserve for the central government the following primary responsibilities: financing, formulation of policies, programming, coverage control, supervision, and quality control. General standards for professional qualification should be set for teachers. Proficiency tests and minimum passing requirements should help ensure quality students.

Delegating Authority

A main characteristic of the current service system is the concentration of responsibilities at the higher levels. The president of the republic must act on such inconsequential administrative issues as appointing teachers in remote areas of the country. In order to improve the efficiency of service delivery, delegating responsibilities is necessary. This should be an integral part of the overall reform of the state.

Entrusting authority to those agencies directly associated with service deliveries would strengthen regional health and education agencies. The most important step for streamlining bureaucratic structures would be to separate planning from service-management functions. Regional offices in charge of service delivery should be allowed to manage a portion of the budget with a degree of freedom and autonomy.

Community Participation: Nongovernmental Organizations

Dominican society has been successful in the delivery of social services through state-subsidized, nongovernmental organizations in the areas of health, social welfare, and university education.

The state does not own or manage the country's most important specialized hospitals. These facilities were built and equipped by civic foundations and trusts that administer the hospitals, not as private for-profit companies but as community facilities. They are not run by the state but have been established as a result of initiatives by specific civic groups that have built and equipped the facilities.

Most of these hospitals receive voluntary donations from companies and individuals, rely on more or less efficient cost-recovery mechanisms, and receive government subsidies. However, since state subsidies are not made on the basis of set policies, the grant amounts depend on the negotiating skill of individual hospital officials and on their ability to convince public health authorities of the facilities' requirements.

The success of private hospital management suggests that some state hospitals could be transferred to social organizations created to assume responsibility for their administration. The government would have to establish criteria to fund these institutions, such as allocating financial resources based on the number of patients cared for in each hospital. Since the current system may not be ready to handle the allocations, financial controls would have to be established.

Trusts created to manage hospitals in the country's relatively small inland cities should include local government and church representatives. If community organizations were responsible for hospital services, it would be easier to determine which households require total subsidy and which can pay part or all of the cost.

Such an arrangement could bring about excellent results in the allocation of social welfare funds. It could also be used in other social programs such as those designed to protect children and the elderly.

BIBLIOGRAPHY

Ceara, M., and E. Croes. 1992. Gasto público social y su impacto en la distribución del ingreso: principales tendencias en la República Dominicana. Santo Domingo: Centro de Investigación Económica para el Caribe (CIECA) and the United Nations Children's Fund (UNICEF). Mimeo.

Díaz Santana, M. 1988. *Situación socioeconómica y formación del magisterio en la República Dominicana*. Santo Domingo: Friedrich Ebert Foundation.

Díaz Santana, M., N. Ramírez, and P. Tactuk. 1990. *Población y educación en la República Dominicana*. Study No. 7. Santo Domingo: Instituto de Estudios de Población de la Asociación Dominicana Pro Bienestar de la Familia.

Lewis, M., M. Sulvetta, and G. Lafogia. 1992. *Public Hospital Costs and Quality in the Dominican Republic*. Working Document (No. 934). Washington, D.C.: The World Bank.

Ramírez, N., I. Duarte, and C. Gómez. 1987. *Población y salud en la República Dominicana*. Santo Domingo: Asociación Dominicana Pro Bienestar de la Familia.

Santana, I., and M. Rathe. 1992. *El impacto distributivo de la gestión fiscal en la República Dominicana*. Santo Domingo: Fundación Siglo 21.

Secretaría de Estado de Educación, Bellas Artes y Cultos (SEEBAC). 1992. Plan decenal de educación. Santo Domingo, Dominican Republic. Mimeo.

United Nations Development Programme (UNDP). 1991. *Desarrollo Humano: Informe 1991*. Bogotá: Editores Tercer Mundo.

CHAPTER FIVE

THREE APPROACHES TO
SOCIAL SERVICE DELIVERY

Cristián Aedo and Osvaldo Larrañaga

This chapter presents a comparative analysis of the case studies described in the preceding chapters. It is based on the findings of the studies (bibliographical references for the individual chapters are the sources for this chapter as well).

The case studies cover three countries with sharply contrasting social policies—Chile, Costa Rica, and the Dominican Republic. The levels of development in Chile and Costa Rica are relatively similar. A per capita gross domestic product (GDP) of roughly $2,000 places both countries in a privileged position within Latin America. As shown in Table 5.1, the social indicators of both countries are well above the average for the rest of the region. One explanation for this achievement is both countries' long history of social development within the context of a political system that favored the systematic integration of emerging social classes. In the early 1970s, the two countries followed different trajectories in their social policies. During that period, a crisis in the system of political integration brought Chile under the rule of an authoritarian government that repudiated the existing social policies. The new regime introduced a set of structural reforms, which dramatically changed Chile's social policies and economic performance a decade earlier than in the rest of the region.

The Dominican Republic presents an entirely different scenario. Relatively underdeveloped, its social indicators fall well below the average for the rest of the region, and the country has no clearly defined social policy. In fact, the Dominican Republic allocates only a small portion of its budget to health, education, and welfare programs and lacks a rational scheme for allocating public funds (see Table 5.2). Coverage of the country's social programs is limited; their institutional framework is unstable; and the country has no social security system in place.

Chile's social policy includes series of innovative measures whose evaluation is indispensable for any reform of the social service delivery system. These measures include decentralization of public health and education services; private sector participation as providers of subsidized education and revenues for

Table 5.1. Economic and Social Indicators, 1990

	Per capita GDP ($US)	Population (Mill.)	Urban Pop. (%)	Life expectancy at birth	Illiteracy rate (%)	Mortality rate[1]	Calories[2]
Chile	1,940	13.2	86	72	7	17	2,581
Costa Rica	1,900	2.8	47	75	7	16	2,808
Dominican Rep.	830	7.1	60	67	17	56	2,356
Latin America	2,171.6	411.3	71.9	67.7	15.3	47.3	2,737

Source: World Development Report 1992, Oxford University Press, World Bank.
Notes: [1] Infant mortality rate, per 1,000 live births.
         [2] Daily caloric intake, per capita, for 1989.

Table 5.2. Spending on Social Programs, 1990
(As a percent of GDP)

	Education Programs	Health	Welfare	Others	Social Spending/ GDP
Chile	2.73	2.14	1.12	10.82	14.02
Costa Rica	4.68	6.30	1.26	8.02	20.20
Dominican Rep.	1.20	1.67	0.10	2.08	5.94

Source: Case studies, respective countries.

other social programs; introduction of cost-recovery schemes in health and higher education; implementation of fiscal transfer mechanisms based on performance criteria; and introduction of subsidized financing for elementary and secondary education.

Costa Rica's social policy is based on a traditional and comprehensive approach to social service delivery. The country allocates a substantial portion of its national budget to the social sector. The figures clearly reflect this orientation: in 1979, the government allocated 10.5 percent of GDP to the health sector and more than 6 percent to education. Although the government was forced to reduce these figures following the crisis of the 1980s, social spending in Costa Rica is clearly higher than in the rest of the region.

Thus Chile and Costa Rica emerge as two alternative regional models for the delivery of social services. The Dominican Republic, for its part, represents in this study an example of the region's poorer countries, where social development is in its early stages and expansion of social programs is urgently needed. The challenge facing these countries will be to develop a social policy that can supplement their emerging economic development.

Education Sector

In general, the private school system is small and caters to high-income students. An exception is the Dominican Republic, where an important segment of tuition-supported private schools serves low-income sectors. These schools operate outside the educational mainstream and are notorious for their poor quality and highly inadequate infrastructure. Their emergence is the result of the public sector's failure to provide adequate services in education.

This dual system of public and private services exists at all levels of higher education in Costa Rica and the Dominican Republic. In Chile, however, public institutions of higher learning are financed largely through tuition fees. They represent in this study the only case of privately funded public education.

Also of interest are publicly funded private services. This is the case in Chile, where subsidized private education accounts for about one third of enrollment at the elementary and secondary levels. The same is true for the traditional private universities founded in Chile before 1980, which receive 50 percent of their income from government contributions.

Table 5.3 presents the principal data for the three countries' educational systems. Coverage in elementary education is practically universal in Chile and Costa Rica. Coverage at the secondary level is 80.2 percent in Chile and 52 percent in Costa Rica. The figure for Costa Rica is lower than its historical standard and represents one of the country's major problems in education. Coverage in elementary and secondary education in the Dominican Republic is 60 percent and 30 percent, respectively. These figures indicate that, increasingly, educational coverage is an important challenge for the country.

The importance of publicly funded education is well-recognized in Chile and Costa Rica. More than 90 percent of all elementary and secondary students in the two countries attend free state-subsidized schools, with private sources providing a large part of Chile's subsidized education. In contrast, figures for the Dominican Republic show the percentage of students in subsidized elementary schools varying between 51 percent and 79 percent, depending on the source. This figure drops to about 32 percent at the secondary level. These statistics once again highlight the insufficient involvement of the state in the country's education sector.

A greater disparity exists in higher education. In Costa Rica, state institutions account for 70 percent of total enrollment, while in Chile and the Dominican Republic the figures are 29 percent and 25 percent, respectively. The apportionment of funds designated to education varies substantially in the three countries. In 1991, the Costa Rican government designated 4.8 percent of GDP for different levels of education (elementary, secondary, and higher). In 1990, Chile allocated 2.35 percent, and the Dominican Republic, 0.67 percent. Clearly,

Table 5.3. Basic Statistics of the Education Sector
(percent)

	Chile	Costa Rica	Dominican Republic
Coverage[1]			
Elementary	90.2	104.0	60.2
Secondary	80.2	52.0	30.0
Higher	11.9	16.0	15.0
Public Education[2]			
Elementary	93.5	94.0	78.0
Secondary	91.9	94.0	31.8
Higher	29.0	70.0	25.0
(universities)	(58.8)	(76.0)	—
Public Spending/GDP			
Elementary	1.31[3]	1.8	0.4
Secondary	0.44[3]	1.0	0.1
Higher	0.60	2.0	0.2
User Contribution			
Elementary	No	No	No
Secondary	No	No	No
Higher	Yes	No	No
Type of subsidy			
Elementary	Demand	Supply	Supply
Secondary	Demand	Supply	Supply
Higher	Mixed	Supply	Supply
Focus[4]			
Elementary	62.6	57.0	52.0
Secondary	51.0	39.0	—
Higher	23.2	—	—

Source: Case studies, respective countries.
Notes: [1] The definition of coverage varies from country to country.
    [2] Registration in public institutions as a percent of total registration.
    [3] Includes subsidized private schools.
    [4] Share of the poorest 40 percent in public spending on the program.

Costa Rica dedicates substantial funds to public education, while Chile allocates more modest funds, and the Dominican Republic provides only small amounts.

Public subsidies generally cover all of the costs involved in education, with no provisions for cost recovery from users. An exception is Chile's university system, which receives about 30 percent of its income from tuition fees and another 20 percent from contracting out applied research and consultancy services. Hence, the state's contribution to public and private universities accounts for approximately half of their budgets.

State subsidies in education are generally provided through grants in Costa Rica and the Dominican Republic. This entails either direct funding of overhead costs (salaries and teacher wages) or, in the case of public universities, transfer of needed financial resources to the entities involved. In Chile, on the other hand, elementary and secondary education is funded through a subsidy system in which individual schools receive a stipend for each student registered. Here we have a decentralized system that uses competition among schools (for attracting students) as an incentive for raising the quality of education. State aid to universities in Chile is delivered in various ways: direct or unrestricted contributions; contributions based on the number of students enrolled in each university; competitive grants for research and development; and student aid programs.

Allocation of public funds hinges on the universal nature of educational programs. In practice, however, self-targeting often occurs since high-income families send their children to tuition-supported private institutions. The impact of government spending, therefore, depends on the socioeconomic background of the students, which, as students move up the educational ladder, is clearly biased toward higher income strata. In this sense, the targeting of public spending depends on the composition of expenditures among the different levels of education. Costa Rica concentrates most of its outlays on higher education (42 percent), while Chile and the Dominican Republic channel their spending mostly toward elementary education (about 55 percent).

It is possible to question the quality of state-supported education in all three countries. In Chile, standardized national test scores of fourth and eighth graders in state-supported schools barely exceed 50 percent, compared to the considerably higher scores of their counterparts in tuition-supported private schools. An even greater disparity exists at the secondary level, as evidenced by scores on college entrance examinations. In Costa Rica, there is also a growing concern over the decline in the quality of education, where fewer than 30 percent of students performed satisfactorily on third and fourth cycle tests. In the Dominican Republic, the problem of quality in public education is compounded by the low-quality education provided by the private sector outside the educational mainstream. Causing great concern are the schools' high dropout and repetition rates and also the fact that many students are older than the norm for their class. The problem of quality also affects the country's university system, which has experienced increased enrollments without improving its infrastructure and academic curricula.

Health Sector

The public health profile of Chile and Costa Rica is similar to that of more developed countries: long life expectancies, low rates of infant mortality and malnutrition, and a low incidence of infectious diseases. This is the result of the two countries' long attention to matters of public health and their high level of education. In contrast, the Dominican Republic's public health profile is similar to that of lesser developed countries: unsatisfactory basic health indicators, poor sanitation, and a high incidence of infectious diseases.

Health systems in the three countries vary considerably. In Chile and Costa Rica, health care services for the poor are exclusively funded from public resources. In the Dominican Republic, the entire health care system is funded this way.

Chile and Costa Rica operate a public health system with mixed funding with outreach through health insurance programs. Both systems provide widespread coverage for the greater part of their populations funded by insurance premiums and supplemental government allocations.[1] On the other hand, the Dominican Republic has a limited health insurance system.

Health insurance is compulsory. In Costa Rica, only public coverage is available. In Chile, however, subscribers can obtain coverage through private health institutions (ISAPRE) by paying a premium. This insurance provides coverage for about 20 percent of the population.

Private insurance coverage is funded and provided by private companies.[2] In the Dominican Republic, companies can obtain private health insurance coverage from private clinics through a mechanism known locally as *igualas*. Private sector providers of health services in the three countries can also treat clients without the use of intermediaries.

Chile's public health system includes private health coverage with payments shared by the clients and the public sector. Beneficiaries can choose any participating private health care provider and pay part of the provider's fee. The Dominican Republic's health care, on the other hand, has an important sector of nongovernmental organizations (NGOs), which are funded by donations, state resources, and foreign aid. The NGOs generally consist of centers qualified to provide specific types of medical services.

The structure of the public health sectors in the three countries varies. Costa Rica has a dual system: the Health Ministry is responsible for formulating policy and for preventive health care and sanitation, while the Social Security Office is in charge of public insurance, medical services, and the country's hospital infrastructure. In Chile the system is more decentralized. The ministry is responsible for formulating policies, medical services are provided by autonomous public service organizations that manage hospitals, and preventive health care is managed by municipalities. In the Dominican Republic, the

---

[1] It should be noted that public financing refers to funds generated from general taxes. Health premiums deposited in the public treasury are classified as private financing.

[2] In principle, private insurance beneficiaries also have access to public institutions.

Table 5.4. Basic Statistics of the Health Sector

	Chile	Costa Rica	Dominican Republic
Coverage[1]			
Public	80.00	90.00	25-35
Private	15.00	—	50-55
Spending/GDP			
Public	2.27	6.30	1.67
Private	1.90[2]	—	—
Spending per beneficiary ($US)			
Public	57.30	140.40	46.00[3]
Private	256.00	—	—
Focus of public spending[4]	52.10	51.20	50-55

Source: Case studies, respective countries.
Notes: [1] Percentage of total population.
[2] Includes only the ISAPRE system.
[3] Assumes 30 percent coverage for public spending and 55 percent for private spending.
[4] Percent channeled to the poorest 40 percent of the population.

health system is centralized. The Undersecretariat of Health is responsible for formulating policy and providing services.

Table 5.4 presents the principal characteristics of coverage and financing of the health care systems in the three countries. Each country's overall system, including both private and public sectors, is shown.

Health coverage is practically universal in Chile and Costa Rica, where more than 90 percent of the population has access to institutional health services. Health services in Costa Rica are provided through the public social security system, which covers 90 percent of the population. The same degree of coverage is provided in Chile through the combined services of public and private insurance (80 percent and 15 percent, respectively).[3] Statistics for the Dominican Republic are less reliable. It is estimated that the actual public health system coverage is between 25 percent and 35 percent, and that only 5 percent of the population subscribes to public insurance. On the other hand, private insurance provides coverage for 25 percent of Santo Domingo's population and between 10 percent and 15 percent of the country's population. Various types of private sector health care services are provided to an estimated 50 percent to 55 percent of the population.

---

[3] The information is for 1990. In 1993, however, private coverage is projected at 25 percent.

An examination of the figures shows that Costa Rica's health care funding is the exception. In fact, Costa Rica allocated 6.7 percent of GDP in 1991 to health care, a figure that largely exceeds the 2.3 percent and 1.7 percent allocated in 1990 by Chile and the Dominican Republic. Even with the inclusion of private sector expenditures in Chile, estimated at 1.9 percent of GDP (including only the ISAPRE program), a disparity in allocations still exists.

An examination of per capita spending on health services offers an interesting perspective. Public per capita outlays in Costa Rica are 2.45 times higher than in Chile and 3.1 times higher than in the Dominican Republic.[4] A comparison of spending between sectors shows that Chile's private sector spends 4.5 times more per beneficiary than its public sector. These figures show that health care in Chile is divided between a private sector that tends to serve the upper-income class and a public sector that caters to the middle class and the poor. The quality of services provided by the two sectors varies significantly. On the other hand, the estimates suggest that per capita spending by the Dominican Republic's private sector is about par with that of the public sector. This does not imply comparable quality in services since those offered by the private sector vary greatly and range from services provided by highly qualified specialty centers to those provided by unqualified, informal ones.

No figures are available on the size of the population segment cared for by Costa Rica's private sector. However, it is clear that nearly the entire population has relatively equal access to a public health care system that allocates a significant amount of resources to the sector. Accordingly, Costa Rica has become a model health care system.

The three health care systems are now at a turning point in their development. Each requires generation of criteria that would provide an adequate framework for future operations. Unless the systems undergo changes, the public health care sector runs the risk of setbacks.

In Costa Rica, the inability of current programs to satisfy new and increasingly complex public demands adequately represents a major challenge for the country. These demands stem from changes in the country's epidemiological profile and in the health care system itself. The problem is partly a financial one (e.g., rising health care prices, increasing population). Ineffective public health management and operations have also created problems. These stem from the division of functions between the Health Ministry and the Social Security Office. Such a system of management is characterized by bureaucratic constraints, power struggles between medical and administrative personnel, excessive hierarchical structures, and a lack of incentives and human resource policies.

---

[4] The figures cover only the part of the population entitled to health coverage. In the Dominican Republic, the estimates are based on 30 percent coverage.

The above problems have impaired the quality of public health care. Increased demand and limited supply have made it necessary to ration services, thus diminishing quality care. The situation has resulted in waiting lines and a reduction in time dedicated to patient care. A spontaneous, and illegal, reaction to the above situation has been the behavior of some doctors who agree to expedite service and provide better care in exchange for additional payments.

A major challenge facing Chile is the poor quality of and limited opportunities for health care in the public health sector. Lack of financial resources accounts for a substantial part of these shortcomings. Low salaries, lack of personnel and equipment, and the deterioration of physical infrastructure are additional problems. These difficulties, while not new, show the enduring cost brought about by years of budgetary constraints. Also contributing to Chile's predicament are serious managerial problems related to rigid labor policies, as well as an institutional reluctance to adopt efficient administrative policies, cost structures, and resource transfers.

The problems of low quality and the high demand for health care that characterize public sector services stand in sharp contrast to the operation of the private ISAPRE program, which provides high-income families with quality and timely health care in a pleasant environment. The disparity between the two sectors puts the equity of the whole system in doubt and has generated strong public opinion in favor of reform.

The main challenge facing the Dominican Republic's public health system is obtaining the necessary resources and improving its efficiency to fulfill its main tasks: to increase coverage and address the population's basic health needs. Moreover, the public system suffers from serious shortcomings, including inefficiency, overcentralization, poor organization, a lack of incentives, etc. As a result, the system needs a strong stimulus to secure the financial, material, and organizational resources necessary to fulfill its mission adequately.

Social Welfare Programs

Social welfare programs are basically assistance programs designed to help the poor and those who lack an income. Viewed more broadly, these programs may include assistance to groups at risk, such as pregnant women, school children, and so on. Assistance programs generally target their efforts toward specific segments of the population.

Social allocations to these programs in Chile and Costa Rica—countries that have had a long involvement in this field—vary between 1 percent and 1.5 percent of GDP. The Dominican Republic, on the other hand, allocates 0.1 percent of GDP to such programs. The Dominican program is fragmented, provides limited coverage, and lacks a defined policy. The fact that the Dominican

Republic's public social security system covers a mere 10 percent of the population is alarming.

Tables 5.5 and 5.6 present information on the major assistance programs discussed here. For the most part, the programs are cash subsidy programs (Family Allowance, Single Family Subsidy [SUF] and Assistance Pensions [PASIS], in Chile; Pensions for the Poor, in Costa Rica); food programs (National Food Subsidy Program [PNAC] and School Food Program [PAE], in Chile; School Lunch in Costa Rica); and comprehensive care programs for children (Child Care Center in Costa Rica). Furthermore, Costa Rica has a program that provides a housing subsidy to poor families to help them become homeowners.[5]

All of the programs mentioned are targeted to specific segments of the population: the elderly, pregnant women, poor children. The only exception is Chile's family allowance program, which provides a subsidy to dependents of social insurance beneficiaries. The amount of the allowance depends on the person's income.

The programs discussed here are quite focused. Except for Chile's family allowance program, the programs' allocations target families in the first two quintile income levels in a ratio greater or equal to two-thirds. In more than half of the cases, such a ratio exceeds 75 percent.

Program targeting mechanisms vary. Financial subsidies in Chile—PASIS and SUF—are determined based on an objective and standardized evaluation of socioeconomic variables related to poverty (CAS record). Beneficiaries must lack formal insurance coverage and be out of work. Financial assistance in Costa Rica—pensions for the poor—targets a similar group. Beneficiaries are selected by social workers through interviews.

School nutrition programs use a different method for identifying beneficiaries. Chile's PAE, for example, uses a two-phase approach. First, the neediest schools are selected based on models that link student groups with their nutritional needs. Teachers from the selected schools then decide which children are to receive assistance. In Costa Rica, selection is made on a geographic basis, with preference given to the poorest areas.

PNAC in Chile targets women who are pregnant or nursing and children under six years of age. The process relies on self-selection. To receive food, people must go to public sector primary health care facilities. The same selection process is also being applied by the Child Care Centers in Costa Rica. These centers provide comprehensive care to children from poor homes in need of nutrition.

In the Chilean case, municipalities are responsible for the SUF, PASIS, and PNAC programs. They select beneficiaries for the financial programs and are

---

5 A similar Chilean program was not included in the study.

Table 5.5. Social Programs: Type of Subsidy and Target Populations

Social programs	Type of Subsidy	Target Population	Benef./ Natl. Pop. (%)	Responsible Entity
Chile (1990)				
Family allowance	Financial	Dependents	29.2	Municipal
PASIS	Financial	Uninsured seniors	2.4	Municipal
SUF	Financial	Uninsured children	5.3	Municipal
PNAC	Food	Children & pregnant women	9.7	Municipal
PAE	Food	Elementary students	4.7	Ministry of Education
Costa Rica (1991)				
School Lunch	Food	Elementary & secondary students	16.1	Ministry of Education
Infant Center	Comprehensive care	Children and the poor	2.1	Ministry of Health
Pension for Indigents	Financial	Seniors and at-risk groups	2.6	Social Security
Housing Subsidy	Financial	Homeless poor families	2.3	Home Mortgage Bank

Source: Case studies, respective countries.

responsible for the programs' administration. Clear advantages are derived from the close ties between program administrators and beneficiaries. PNAC food deliveries are made through primary care facilities that are also run by municipalities.

The Costa Rican case presents an interesting means of funding assistance programs. The nation's Social Development and Family Allowance Fund (FODESAF) finances the bulk of the programs described. The fund, in turn, pays for specific programs through taxes. In this way, welfare program funding is shielded from arbitrary interventions, yet is subject to the business cycle.

Table 5.6. Social Programs: Spending Comparisons

Social Programs	Spending/ GDP	Per Capita annual (US$) spending	Focus (%)	Focusing Mechanism
Chile (1990)				
Family allowance	0.40	43	43.3	Income
PASIS	0.41	17	67.7	CAS record
SUF	0.10	43	80.0	CAS record
PNAC	0.16	46	79.7	self-exclusion
PAE	0.09	77	68.9	Schools and teachers
Costa Rica (1991)				
School Lunch	0.20	22	74.4	Geographical
Infant Center	0.20	272	76.3	Nutritional risk
Pension for indigents	0.20	167	64.3	Social work evaluation
Housing Subsidy	0.50	2,916	75.6	Questionnaire

Source: Case studies, respective countries.

Policy Lessons

Funding and Sustainability of Social Policy

In the cases examined, Chile seems to have the most solid social policy base. In fact, the country relies on fiscal revenues derived from a broad and mature tax base that is strengthened by a stabilization fund endowed with income generated by copper exports. Expansion of fiscal income is supported by an average annual economic growth of 7 percent. This allows expansion of tax revenues of around 10 percent per year. Equally important is a broad political consensus in supporting social programs. The consensus has enabled a strengthening of these programs through such initiatives as the 1990 tax reform.

The situation in Costa Rica is more ambivalent. The country's social programs represent an important, internationally acclaimed achievement in program coverage and development. Social policy is a national priority. Furthermore, the country does not have a defense budget, avoiding a costly and rigid budgetary allocation. However, rising costs of social service provision have recently created serious fiscal problems. In this regard, supporting social policies will require a structural adjustment between revenues and fiscal expenditures.

In the Dominican Republic, funding and supporting a social policy is even more critical. Financial allocations over the years have been clearly insufficient and inconsistently allocated to the sector. Despite the country's high level of poverty, virtually no social security program or welfare budgets have been established. This reflects the absence of a social policy and the government's lack of concern for social policy issues. To redress this problem, the Dominican Republic first needs to commit itself to developing a social policy program and then strengthening the tax base so that it can create and implement the program.

Decentralization

The study highlights the Chilean experience in the decentralization of health, education, and welfare programs. Costa Rica and the Dominican Republic, however, retain traditional centralized programs that are afflicted by predictable shortcomings. These failures include poor suitability to local needs, rigidity, inertia, and hierarchical decision making. However, Chile's decentralization has also had its share of problems. Its findings can serve as a test case in the future decentralization of other social programs.

Indeed, decentralization of Chile's education and health care sectors has been more a formality than a reality. Only a small percentage (18 percent) of schools have adapted their curricula to reflect changes in population or geographic environment. Most schools have chosen to adopt a centralized model promoted by the ministry. In practice, health care services also continue to be centralized, even in those areas where they are legally autonomous.

A lack of personnel training and motivation helps explain this situation. There are no specific incentives that reward superior management in education and health care. Dynamic and independent-minded people have traditionally sought employment in the private sector, which offered them a more favorable environment for developing their capabilities and interests. Labor rigidities have also contributed to undermining the autonomy of social service providers. The government has allowed such rigidities as a way to compensate for the low wages of workers in public health and education.

Another factor that has hampered Chile's decentralization process has been its political environment. Indeed, decentralization was carried out for the first 10 years under an authoritarian regime that centralized policy decisions, restricted participation by local communities in providing public services, and limited the actual degree of provider autonomy.

The decentralization of financial subsidy programs in Chile has had positive results. In fact, municipalities have generally been efficient in their tasks of identifying and selecting beneficiaries and managing the programs. General guidelines for program selection and funding are drawn up at the central level. The scheme constitutes an effective division of labor between public authorities based on comparative advantages.

Fiscal Transfer Mechanisms

Transfers of public resources to social service providers are, generally, centrally controlled (through direct government financing) or occur through fund transfers based on existing or negotiated procedures.

The Chilean case provides several new approaches in this area. Specifically, public funds for elementary and secondary education are channeled through a subsidy system whereby schools receive a stipend for each student enrolled. In this way, schools compete to attract students by offering higher quality education. However, pressures from teacher associations and other sector members have limited the impact of this type of subsidy as a competitive mechanism by restricting parental access to standardized national test results, which would provide information about individual schools' performance.

The Chilean study includes an econometric evaluation of the quality of elementary education, which uses scores from these tests as dependent variables. This evaluation shows that students in subsidized private schools perform better than their counterparts in municipal schools, after controlling for the impact of the socioeconomic and resource-base variables. This result confirms that private subsidized schools are funded more efficiently than municipal schools. Besides, competition is more open among private subsidized schools.

Chile has also adopted a retroactive payment system in the health care sector (with payments based on results). However, the operation of this system has not been compatible with planned fiscal budgets and has relied, in practice, on existing and negotiated criteria for allocating funds to the health system.

Costa Rica presents an interesting use of tax revenues that are specifically allocated to FODESAF. While this type of financing is procyclical, its structure ensures resources for high-impact poverty programs. Ideally, schemes should be designed similar to the stabilization mechanisms that rely on revenues derived from primary commodity exports, but they should be of an anticyclical nature. Yet, higher education in Costa Rica provides an example of entitlements that are constitutionally guaranteed and protected from arbitrary cuts. This approach could be criticized from the standpoint of equity since protecting the budget for higher education requires shortchanging those for elementary and secondary education.

Targeting

Chile and Costa Rica provide interesting examples in targeting public spending. Targeting in these countries has generally been adequate and has been applied to effective monetary subsidy and school lunch programs. Targeting has entailed a protracted effort aimed at perfecting the means of implementing programs.

The findings in these countries indicate that targeting requires a learning process. This represents a necessary investment that results in the development of an effective social policy. An important by-product is the development of information systems, which are particularly useful during periods of crisis, when peak efficiency is required of social programs.

The countries discussed here share a common perspective in the education and health care sectors. The public sector shall provide universal elementary and secondary education, as well as preventive and curative health care. Universal coverage is a reality in Chile and Costa Rica, while in the Dominican Republic it is only an objective that, in view of the country's limited social policy progress, is yet to be achieved.

In Chile and Costa Rica, targeting is carried out through self-selection in education, whereby the wealthier segment of the population enrolls its children in tuition-supported private schools. In the Dominican Republic, a portion of the country's poor are educated in cheaper, less-qualified, tuition-supported schools because they lack public school alternatives.

In health care, on the other hand, targeting through self-selection is well-known in Chile, where an extensive private health insurance system exists. In Costa Rica, health care demand is concentrated in the public sector due, in part, to the relatively high quality of the public health system, and, in part, to the absence of private insurance programs.

Private Delivery Systems

The most important findings highlighted in this study concerning private delivery of social services relate to elementary and secondary education in Chile. Here, the private and public (municipality) sectors compete through the previously mentioned subsidy system. The competition is carried out on a large scale since the private subsidized sector accounts for more than a third of the enrollment in publicly funded schools. The Chilean study also shows that, after controlling for the impact of other variables, such a system has achieved quality standards superior to those of municipal institutions. Hence, subsidized private sector education has made a positive contribution to Chile's education system.

Findings in totally private (not subsidized) deliveries of social services offer an interesting insight. These services have had an impact on those provided by public entities.

In the Chilean case, the providers of private health care insurance (ISAPRE) have induced important changes in public health care. It has been shown that a public system with internal redistribution schemes is inconsistent with a private system that provides benefits based on subscriber premiums. Indeed, the ISAPRE system was responsible for the massive exodus from the public system of high-income subscribers who were subsidizing the poorer beneficiaries in the system. Rising labor demand in the private system has also caused medical and paramedical workers to expect higher salaries. As a consequence, Chile's public health service is faced with the dual challenge of increasing labor costs while coping with diminishing revenues.

In the Dominican Republic, the private sector has filled the void created by the government's failure to provide social services. Hence, the institution of *igualas*, or private health insurance, has gained great acceptance in the mainstream urban sector. Moreover, there has been widespread use of services provided by private health care and educational suppliers outside the mainstream and in the marginal urban sector. These services, however, have been of inferior quality and have been provided under conditions that fail to meet minimum health and education requirements.

Finally, Costa Rica has developed the provision of health services in the public system (*biombos*). Patients wanting better, more timely care make illegal payments to doctors who take advantage of the system. This practice reflects the shortcomings of the public health system and the willingness of people to pay for better-quality services. The authors of the Costa Rican study suggest that the solution to this problem lies in a public sector offering of two types of services based on different standards of "luxury." These offerings would provide services of equal quality, thus preserving the tradition of universal public health coverage in that country. The situation might also reflect the need for a private insurance system that would satisfy demands by subscribers who are willing to pay more for better-quality services.

An additional issue related to private social services is the need for public regulation. This consideration was instrumental in creating a Superintendency for ISAPRE in Chile and has motivated a debate on the need to require accreditation for institutions of higher education.

Cost Recovery

In the cases of Chile and Costa Rica, health care programs are largely financed through monthly premiums paid by subscribers. Chile also uses a supplementary fee-for-service system (co-payment). This system combines efficiency and equity in treating at-risk subscribers since fee amounts depend on subscriber income.

Also of interest is Chile's system of higher education. This system receives fiscal contributions that partially subsidize teaching staffs. However, enrollment fees account for a substantial portion of university funding. In Costa Rica and the Dominican Republic, on the other hand, cost recovery is practically nonexistent. Consequently, public support of higher education subsidizes middle- and upper-class students. The problem is that such financial support is not really justifiable in terms of efficiency or equity, and it competes with fiscal resources that could be allocated to programs that yield greater social returns.

INDEX

Adjustment program, Dominican Republic, 92
Agency-principal problem, 4
Albretch, D., 4n.2
Allen, J.W., 7
Assaél, J., 13n.2
Assistance pensions (PASIS), Chile, 28, 31, 42, 136–37

Barr, N., 7
Becker, G.S., 8
Behrman, J., 8
Beneficiaries
  Dominican Republic: of public spending on education, 113–14
  household assessment of social programs, 8
  self-selection effect, 6
  views of, 4–5
Besley, T., 6
Biombo system, Costa Rica, 59, 63
Birdsall, N., 5
Blackorby, C., 6
Blank, R., 2
Brakarz, J., 3
Budinich, E., 13n.1

Campbell, T., 3
Casassus, J., 13n.2
CASEN survey, Chile. *See* Socioeconomic profile survey (CASEN), Chile

Castañeda, T., 13nn1,2
CCSS. *See* Social Security Fund (CCSS), Costa Rica
Ceara, M., 113
Centralization
  Costa Rica: problems of, 60–61
  Dominican Republic: of SESPAS services, 99, 114–17
CEPAL. *See* Comisión Económica para América Latina (CEPAL)
Chibber, A., 1
Child Care Program, Costa Rica, 78–79, 81–83, 136–37
Children
  Chile: programs for, 27–30
  Costa Rica: Child Care Program, 78–79, 81–83, 136–37
  Dominican Republic: child welfare, 115–16
Civil service, Chile, 25
Clinics and centers
  Chile: for delivery of primary health care, 20, 30
  Costa Rica: cooperative, 62
Coate, S., 6
Cohen, E., 75n.5
Comisión Económica para América Latina (CEPAL), 85
Community participation, Dominican Republic, 124–25
Competition, Chile, 16, 45, 131